All the praise and glory to God Almighty for my testimony in the journey that has occurred and yet to come.

Contents

Chapter One ~ Hello, Ted

I never imagined how drastically life would change. No one imagines going through a medical journey that takes you through bends and curves through winding roads reaching mountain peaks and nestled valleys. The journey is ever moving and can ebb and flow like a roaring river just to reach a calm flowing stream and repeat the cycle again. No, I wasn't prepared for any of this. Not physically, mentally, emotionally, or spiritually. God never discusses His plans with us, but when He unveils His works, they are truly awe inspiring and when you accept them, it's a place you can imagine not being able to go.

Nickolas, my bonus son, loved the Beatles and we were all privy to his selection of musical genre through his teen years, but this band created a kindred spirit as I loved them just as much. Nickolas could tell me facts he had discovered that maybe I didn't know. He read books, musical highlights, articles, played rifts on his guitar, and jammed to them while doing homework, riding in the car, or sang them wherever he went. I didn't realize the Christmas of 2018, when I penned the inscription of his newly acquired Beatles book detailing my plans for us to see Paul McCartney Memorial Day 2019, that it would be an event that would change us all.

Nickolas and I arrived at PNC in Raleigh, North Carolina stoked with anticipation and capturing photos before the concert began. We enjoyed some food and drinks and found our seats. Those seats were high, not far from the top of the arena. The seats were not the most comfortable for my curvy frame, but I was going to make the best of it no matter my fear of heights or plus sized overflow in the chair. We took Snapchats and videos. We screamed, we sang, we were in just plain awe. I looked over and saw this sweet child I had come to love as my own enjoying a dream come true moment. It was a priceless moment I will never forget, and my camera caught a glance of it to memorialize. At the conclusion of the concert, I asked Nickolas to wait until everyone left, so I wouldn't take a chance at falling. Stop right there. See that was MY plan, but God had other plans. We waited and as soon as I exited and took a step down. BOOM. I fell. I remember struggling to hold onto the railing, so I wouldn't tumble down. I never hit my head and Nickolas rushed to see if I was ok. Of course, I was embarrassed that my almost- forty-year-old self-had fallen. I took a minute to catch my breath. I shook it off and we exited the venue. I drove us home even though I was abruptly sore from the fall. I laid down and asleep I went.

The next day, you can imagine how sore I was. I could not move without pain striking my body. I called Mama, my grandma, and she suggested I go into the local emergency room to ensure I had not broken any ribs or hit my head. I hesitated thinking I would be fine. I just needed a hot bath, a heating pad, and some Tylenol. She persisted and I finally caved. Nickolas drove me to the emergency room mid-morning, and I was seen by the physician's assistant. They ordered a CT scan to make sure I had not hit my head. He returned to my room and in the fog of it all, he said "You have a mass on your brain not related to your fall". I couldn't even conceive the words he uttered. I just kept saying "What do you mean?" He stated there was at CT scan on file from 2014, where Cameron, my husband, and I were in a motorcycle accident, they compared it to. Back then, there was a pimple on my brain. A pimple!!! What on earth is this man talking about! What is he saying!!! He ordered an MRI. I immediately called Cameron and my Mama, crying exclaiming "I have a mass on my brain". Nickolas had to be at work and he stayed until they came. I cannot imagine if he realized just what they were saying and to be honest, we never have spoken of it. The whirlwind that followed erased any chances to prepare my children, biological or bonus.

That MRI! I was already panicked and unnerved because I just could not process what was going on. Then they wanted me to climb into this tiny machine for at least thirty minutes. I was in sheer agony. The anxiety had wrapped itself around me like a coiled snake. I couldn't breathe. The medical staff gave me medication and my body responded in the opposite direction. I was more amped up and terrified. Just the most agonizing and probably the most dramatic tears the medical staff had seen were sliding down my cheeks. My Mama and husband, Cameron were just like get in the machine. I went in. I never made it past ten minutes. I crawled out of it. Literally. I just could not do it. I was flashed with heat and wanted to go outside. Everything was caving in on me. I wanted to RUN. I wanted to run away from it all. This was NOT happening! Even outside, I thrashed about through tears and my own rational thinking that by now anxiety had riddled with irrationality. I went back in and made up my mind. I was not staying there. I wanted out. I needed out now. So, I left AMA (against medical advice) even after the medical team offered to admit me and reattempt the MRI again. No! No! No! Let me out!...AND out I went.

I went home to sleep off the medication they gave me. I was nauseous, jittery, and the world was spinning. The children, Gracie, Riley, and Ashleigh had no idea why I was in this state. They'd never seen me like this. It must have been frightening. I cried for I don't know how long. I calmly met Cameron on the couch and simply said "I don't want to know. Let's not worry about it. I don't want to know what is going on. Let it play out and let me enjoy the rest of my life, with whatever time I have left and just not know." I think back now, and I sob. What my poor husband must have felt in that moment. He just let me talk. We both knew I had an appointment with a new general practitioner at the new healthplex in town, and I would have to face it then, but today. I was going to run, and I ran in what seemed like circles. Circles of thoughts in my head, spinning, like I was in an abyss. Falling without any end in sight.

I met my new practitioner, and she ordered another MRI in Greenville, North Carolina, along with a consult with their neurologist. She listened. Really listened. She had copies of the MRI from the emergency department and said without the contrast version, the scans could not definitively give her answers. I dropped my head facing the inevitable truth, I would have to go back in this machine and get answers I probably didn't want to hear. I was scheduled for a Saturday appointment. My Dad and Gail, my stepmom, had Ashleigh as Cameron drove me to Greenville, North Carolina. My doctor had prescribed me medication to take for my anxiety and to keep me calm in the MRI. Who knew anxiety caused an intense rush of claustrophobia? She had listened so keenly, and I took the medication. They even allowed Cameron to hold me hand during the scan while they played music on the headphones placed gently over my head. The noises from the machine were almost drowned out. After thirty minutes, I was done. A copy would be forwarded to my doctor for a follow-up appointment. Cameron and I went to Red Robin that night for an early dinner. I don't remember much of it. The medication I had taken made me so drowsy. I never complained about the wrong order I had received. He said I ate it and seemed to enjoy it. Years later, we laugh because among all this I was calm and during dinner we never discussed what was happening. He just tells me I smiled a lot.

The follow-up to my doctor concluded that the mass on my brain was indeed a brain tumor. A meningioma. The best kind of brain tumor to get if you get one. It was over 4 cm. My referral to the neurologist concluded that surgery or stereostactic radiation would be possible to remove it. In breaking the news to my Aunt Pam, I reached out to her for a second opinion. My Google research concluded tumors this size didn't do well under stereostactic radiation. I sent my information to her colleague at Duke. She forwarded my information to my now neurosurgeon. After much debate, it was determined the tumor would need to be removed via a craniotomy. First, I had to come in for my consultation. Again, Mama and Cameron attended the appointment. To this day, I don't remember a lot that was said other than I had to have surgery, these are the risks, and this is what will happen if you don't. The latter was scarier than having the surgery. How in the world did I miss this? How did I miss the signs? Why didn't the doctor who read my CT scan suggest follow up? Why didn't my doctor then suggest I follow up? Why....Why....Why? God, WHY!!!!

I broke the news to extended family, friends, and church family. I had kept much of this unknown to the younger children because I wanted to have the exact details when I told them. Their precious faces were filled with fear. Yet, they said nothing. They gave us hugs and told me how much they loved me. They worried quietly as we adults ran to and fro trying to carry on with normal life. How much I wish I could have gone back and slowed down for them.

Cameron tried to make the best of those days leading up to the surgery. We had day dates on Saturday, and I recall giving him instructions for my funeral. I told him where, what I wanted to wear, what songs I wanted sung/played, who I wanted to sing them, and what scripture I wanted said. I absolutely believed I wouldn't make it through this. I was so anxious, and it triggered depression. Feelings like I had not felt. Sure, I had been sad, but not hopeless. He just simply asked me not to talk like that. It was going to be ok, and he was right, but I couldn't see it. No one could make me see it. My Mama, my sister, Brandie, my Dad, or Gail. I literally thought I was doomed. This was my time, and I was going to have to accept leaving those I loved. I was distraught.

I was at work, when I probably should have been at home, but I have always been one to dedicate myself, all of myself, to my job. It was no different. This was my team, and I adored the members on it. We had been through so much since our inception in February 2018. I broke the news to them and my supervisor. I think astonishment was a fitting description, but my supervisor and I took it in stride. We named the tumor Ted. Ted the Tumor. It wasn't like it was a Ted around that I didn't like. It just suited the phrase... the tumor. We had a countdown on my office door, whereby we changed the number each day to signify that Ted had to go. I threw myself into my work to avoid dealing with it all. I wanted everything left for others to do in order. I left precise instructions on how to handle each situation and instructions on how I did my day-to-day routine. I wanted to make sure I left my house in order.

We had come upon the month of June through this. Not even a month had passed since that fateful day in May. Our anniversary had occurred. It was quiet and at a local restaurant. I can't remember if we even exchanged gifts then. Those weeks were like a blur. Gracie's birthday was just days before my surgery. I had to make sure we celebrated it. We had purchased a new bicycle for her. We invited friends from church and our immediate family. She enjoyed herself, but I look back on those photos and I see me holding on with everything I have got. That smile not even really one. Just one plastered on my face for my bonus baby's big day.

Pre-Op. The lengths of what it entailed for this surgery dumbfounded me. Sure, I'd had a C-section, it was even emergent, but it didn't require the labs, cardiac tests, measurement of my head, portable X-ray, etc. before I even checked in the night before. The team of doctors came down to the waiting area of the hospital and told me it appeared the tumor was trying to attach to my optic nerve, and I could potentially lose my eyesight. First, I was prepared to lose my sense of smell through this surgery, but to add potential blindness I just could not fathom. My neurosurgeon's assistant wheeled me into the elevator, through hallways, and corridors to my room. Cameron alongside me as they guided me. He never left me. The nurse directed me to wash with antibacterial soap and prepare for the IV upon completion. The IV was inserted and I had to have a mapping MRI. It would be used the next day to precisely cut into the brain and remove the tumor. I can't say I didn't panic because I did. Yet, I was assured I would be given medication, and just like the one in Greenville, it was better than what I expected. I returned to my room where Cameron was waiting. Nursing staff checked on me routinely. I'm not sure how either of us got any sleep. Cameron left the television on all night playing contemporary Christian music. Surgery was early the next morning and God knew I needed peace.

I arose the next morning with medical staff, what seemed like ten at a time, talking to me about what the day would be like. I was wheeled down to the pre-op room and my family was allowed to visit. Two at a time, they visited. My Mama came in and I'm sure uttered a prayer over me with such faith that it could move a mountain. My Uncle JB, Mama's brother, came to tell me good luck. His wife had undergone something similar in the 1980s and his support has never waivered since learning the news. My sister, Brandie and my pastor, Daryl was there in attendance to support not only me, but Cameron. My Dad and Gail came in before I was whisked off to surgery and I remember my father holding my hand and I just cried. You see we lost my mother in 2007 due to medical issues and Dad always made sure to tell us that we needed to keep up with physicals. Her loss twelve years earlier had been extremely hard on him, and I can't begin to even understand what thoughts he had going through his mind to think he might lose a child.

They wheeled me into a room just outside the OR and administered medication.... and I was out. Cameron described the longest hours drumming by. By the time I woke up and fully gained my faculties, I was in Neuro-ICU, protocol post-surgery. A piece of metal had dropped into my eye and the ophthalmologist attempted to flush it out to prevent further injury was one of my first memories. My head was bound so tightly. I had on oxygen, but I was alive. I made it. Of course, Brandie had to test out my sense of smell by breathing in my face asking if I could smell it. It hurt to laugh. Uncle JB was amazed I was doing so well. Daddy and Gail were relieved. Pastor Daryl had been there all day with Cameron and the family. The prayers I can only imagine that were prayed that day still bring tears to my eyes. The next couple of days I remained in the hospital and was discharged home with lengthy instructions.

Cameron was up around the clock to pass medications, put a pack of frozen peas on my head, and to just listen. He had an air mattress next to the couch. If I moved, he was there. Sometimes, he held my hand until I went to sleep. He kept a watchful eye over me. He changed bandages, which are not his favorite especially with my long hair, he showered me, and he dressed me. He made sure I ate. Still, I fell in a depression like one I have never seen. It wasn't as dark those first weeks, but anxiety held me captive. I had no idea what lay ahead.

Chapter Two ~ Welcome to 40!

I got my staples out in early July. Things seemed to be progressing well. I was getting out and weened off medication I no longer needed. Some normalcy seemed to be creeping outward, but anxiety always lay there ready to suit up and build an outward armor against any rationality and faith. I began reading the book of Psalms on the advisement of Pastor Daryl, then Proverbs. Then, I decided I'd read the New Testament. Yet, looking back, my faith was like a small shoot growing and the soil was somewhere between rocky and sandy. It fighting to take root. I posted pictures throughout the days and weeks, but I woke up one morning and there was swelling. It shifted the next day to the other side. I planned to contact the neurosurgeon on Monday. I dressed for church, my first visit back, and amid the service, I felt sick. Cameron and I left and went home. Unbeknownst to me, I had a pseudomonas infection. Mama and I went to the Duke- Raleigh emergency department. A CT scan was completed, and the result showed an edema. Follow-up was scheduled with the neurosurgeon. At the visit, he was very concerned as he saw symptoms of infection in my scar line and proceeded to insert a needle to withdraw fluid. I had missed it! It was trickling back into my long curly hair, and I had no idea. There was no anesthesia and Mama was required to sit as far as possible from me. The nurse held my hand during the procedure. We waited for results and waited. Finally, the results came back, and it had not grown anything in the lab. I was released and Mama drove me home. We discussed my birthday plans for the next day. I was turning 40 and she was making my favorite birthday meal- fried chicken, all the fixins, and homemade chocolate cake. Now, this chocolate cake recipe has been passed down since my paternal great-grandmother, Mary Edwards. I almost think it may have come over on the boat with our ancestors. It is one of the cakes Mama makes that I truly love.

I woke up to forty on July 24th. Sure, I was a month in after my craniotomy. I was healing. My hair was growing back, and I was looking forward to finding the normal in my life. I was thanking God each day for this blessing of life. The children and I were going to Mama's for lunch to meet my sister, Brandie, and enjoy the festivities of being forty. Yeah, it wasn't the fortieth birthday party I imagined, but I was alive. I was blessed to find this unknown tumor, Ted, and have him removed successfully. I mean after all, the neurosurgeon believed he had gotten it all within reason. You can't account for microscopic cells. So, I was counting down to my next MRI and to be cleared from the doctor. The swelling had gone down on my face since the day before. So, when the phone rang, I saw the caller ID and knew it wasn't going to be good news. The doctor on the neurosurgeon's team stated I had an infection and surgery must happen today. "How quickly can you get to Duke?". I stammered and explained I would need to pack a bag and call my husband, but we would be there soon. I called Mama and we agreed she would take the children. My birthday meal was nearly done. My sister would be there soon. I called Cameron at work and explained he needed to come home. I needed to get to Duke for surgery. I cried out to God! Why me Lord? The song I had grown to love was now the cry to God because I didn't understand His plan. I didn't understand why this was happening. I thought we were done. Hadn't I grown these mustard seeds of faith? Weren't they sprouting up? Didn't He see the shoots in the ground? I'm 40! I'm supposed to be celebrating.

Cameron arrived at home and whisked me to Duke. We both had bags packed knowing we would be there a few days. I reported to the clinic to get the pre-op completed just like I had done the month before. Medical staff realized it was my birthday and told me happy birthday. The receptionist even made me a card at her desk. All the while, my children, sister, and Mama were celebrating my birthday meal without me. The tears were here, there, and everywhere. The medical team was compassionate. They knew what the neurosurgeon was seeking in the labs ordered. I just didn't.

I was led to the pre-op room and the nurses had to take blood gases from my feet. It was the most painful thing I had experienced. She put her phone on Christian contemporary music and I mouthed the words to the songs that played while tears streamed down my face. I was lost. I was in the abyss again and this time, I felt so alone. What mustard seeds? The sprouts were wilted and not growing. The neurosurgeon's assistant stated they would take out my bone flap, debride the area, and possibly leave it out to be replaced at a later date six months down the road. I was horrified. No forehead! What do you mean!?!?! Cameron had to calm me down. They took me to the OR. I was shifted from the gurney to the OR gurney. I remember counting and then nothing.

When I awoke, I was sweating and on fire. I still had my forehead. They had debrided the area, removed the bone flap, and cleaned it, and then returned it back. I was there in that tiny bed trembling and trying desperately to find something to alleviate this. I had soaked the linens in my bed. The poison in my body being released. Tylenol for pain and waiting on a room. I was in agony. It felt like I had been outside on the hottest days of July and returned to no air conditioning with no relief. Cameron tried his best to help me. They transferred me to a room and there I lay. Silent. I wept. I was lost and I felt alone. Cameron played my Christian music, but I could not find the joy in this journey. I was defeated. I could not joke. I could barely talk to my sister, Brandie, when she called. My voice was hollow. No emotion. I was truly hopeless, and I didn't want to fight this fight anymore.

My sister, Brandie, stopped by on her way to her planned vacation. She tried to joke with me that she ate my birthday cake. Mama had brought me a slice, along with Riley and Gracie for a visit., but I couldn't eat it. I couldn't face my children. I was awake, but I wasn't there. I slipped into a depression of the likes I had never experienced. In all my years of work in the field of mental health and developmental disabilities, I never expected to be the one that would be this broken. My heart was shattered. I should know all the signs and be able to cope better. I mean I had taught people coping skills for years. How could I be affected by depression?! I was. Its grip was so tight on me it nearly suffocated me.

The Infectious Disease team came in and informed me about the type of infection I had. It was a little too much information. I had a team of ten staring at me in the bed with two IVs, both full of high-powered antibiotics and fluids, telling me how this type of infection can be resistant. I finally asked, "Am I going to die? Will this kill me?". They replied no, I didn't have that kind. They explained I would go home on a PICC line and would have antibiotic care for six weeks.

I was hospitalized until discharge plans had been rendered. My medicine would be dropped off the day of my discharge at home. There's no one in the world who could have prepared me for that PICC line procedure. It had to be sterile. I had to limit my movements. Anxiety does not allow for that to happen, but those wonderful professionals! How amazing those folks were at Duke. I knew they were amazing the first time, but this time they showed so much care in their movements and their words. I had so many requirements that needed to be done to ensure I didn't get an infection in the line. I was terrified so much I was literally afraid to live. I was afraid to talk about it that I might cause attention to it and the attention would lead to more problems to occur.

When I returned home, the depression sank even further. It was a spider web I felt evermore trapped in day after day. Mama and Cameron tried their best to understand it all. My local doctor suggested medication and I finally agreed. I had wept until my face felt like it had blistered from the tears. I wept in her office, at home, and at the drop of anything. My thoughts were surrounded by how was I going to get through this, why was I going through this, and what had I done to deserve God's wrath? Day after day, Cameron and Mama rotated giving me my medication three times a day. We had it down like clockwork. I was obsessively protective over the PICC line to ensure it did not get tangled or wet while I was being showered. Everything had to be clean. I couldn't afford to get another infection.

My home health nurse brought the sunshine in my life on her visits. I nearly fainted while she tried to change out my line. I do not do well with needles, procedures, etc. I was so anxious all the time, I am not sure how I kept any wits about myself. For four weeks, she came faithfully, and she always encouraged me to find my faith. I looked forward to my visits with her. I kept reading my Bible. Page after page as I read of how Jesus had healed others. I would listen to my Christian music in my bed, day after day, and weep. Not just cry, but sob to Him. I would weep until I was exhausted. I would pray and cling to those words. When I couldn't find the words to pray, I wept. I held my Bible sometimes until I fell asleep. I was exhausted from this journey.

I had experienced a fever one night. I had chills and I knew something was not right. My body was signaling that something was wrong again. The labs the home health nurse drew would provide the clues and another telephone call.

Chapter Three~ I'm Not a Warrior

I received a call that day in August 2019 from Infectious Disease, indicating there was something amiss. I reported to the emergency department that day at Duke. I called Mama and told her I needed to go and asked if she would take me this time. Of course, she obliged. Cameron remained with the children and prepared them for back-to-school the following week. I needed them to have one of us and to have something normal to cling to. Their entire summer was full of my medical mishaps, my depression, and my withdrawal from them. Ashleigh, my daughter with Autism, couldn't understand what was happening and the more I withdrew; the more confused she became. Riley, my son, was worried. He developed anxiety and worried over me constantly. Gracie, my bonus daughter, remained quiet. Just like her Dad, Cameron, and worried in secret. Nickolas, my bonus son, kept busy and stayed strong for them I imagine. He was the eldest of all four at home. It's his nature. So, Mama drove, and we arrived early evening to a bustling emergency room filled with all sorts of people with all sorts of ailments.

Finally, I was called back, and the battery of tests began. They were not sure if the PICC line had become infected. How could this be? I had taken every single precaution to keep infection at bay. I slept with a different pillowcase each night that my arm and head rested on. I had kept the area covered when showering to ensure no moisture was able to penetrate. I kept myself isolated from others most of the time. I spent a night and half the next day until a room was ready. I heard everything from mobile X-ray to spinal tap. I shook with fear and my Mama prayed. She sat in the straight back chair and prayed. I don't know the words she said, but I knew the look on her face. I found some sleep off and on, but I was uncomfortable on that small bed. I was awakened as the emergency department team, neurosurgeon team, and infectious disease team worked around the clock to figure out what was going on. I was transferred to a room for further care.

Those days were full of the worst anxiety. Doctors came to and fro. Nursing staff came in and out. Vitals were checked. Blood was drawn. The Cefepime was stopped and my PICC line was no longer used. Infectious Disease finally determined no growth for infection had occurred, but I was neutropenic. My white blood count was 0.5. I was vulnerable to everything. Before COVID, my doctors and nursing staff were wearing masks to protect me from the least scary of germs. I was susceptible to the common cold, and it could be deadly. I stayed until my numbers improved enough to go home. It was a total of three nights and four days. Mama drove me home. I had missed open house for school and purchasing school supplies. The children showed me their purchases and how eager they were to start school the following week. I was gripped by fear. The fear of the unknown. I had an MRI coming up and I automatically believed I was destined to lose this battle. There was no need to make future plans. I would not be able to win this war. My battle cry was silenced as I slipped the armor off and sat there. I didn't want to try or push forward. I was worn out. The ambitious woman sat defeated. I wasn't the same woman I had been before. I didn't recognize my own reflection. The tattered scar line that had been carved out twice,

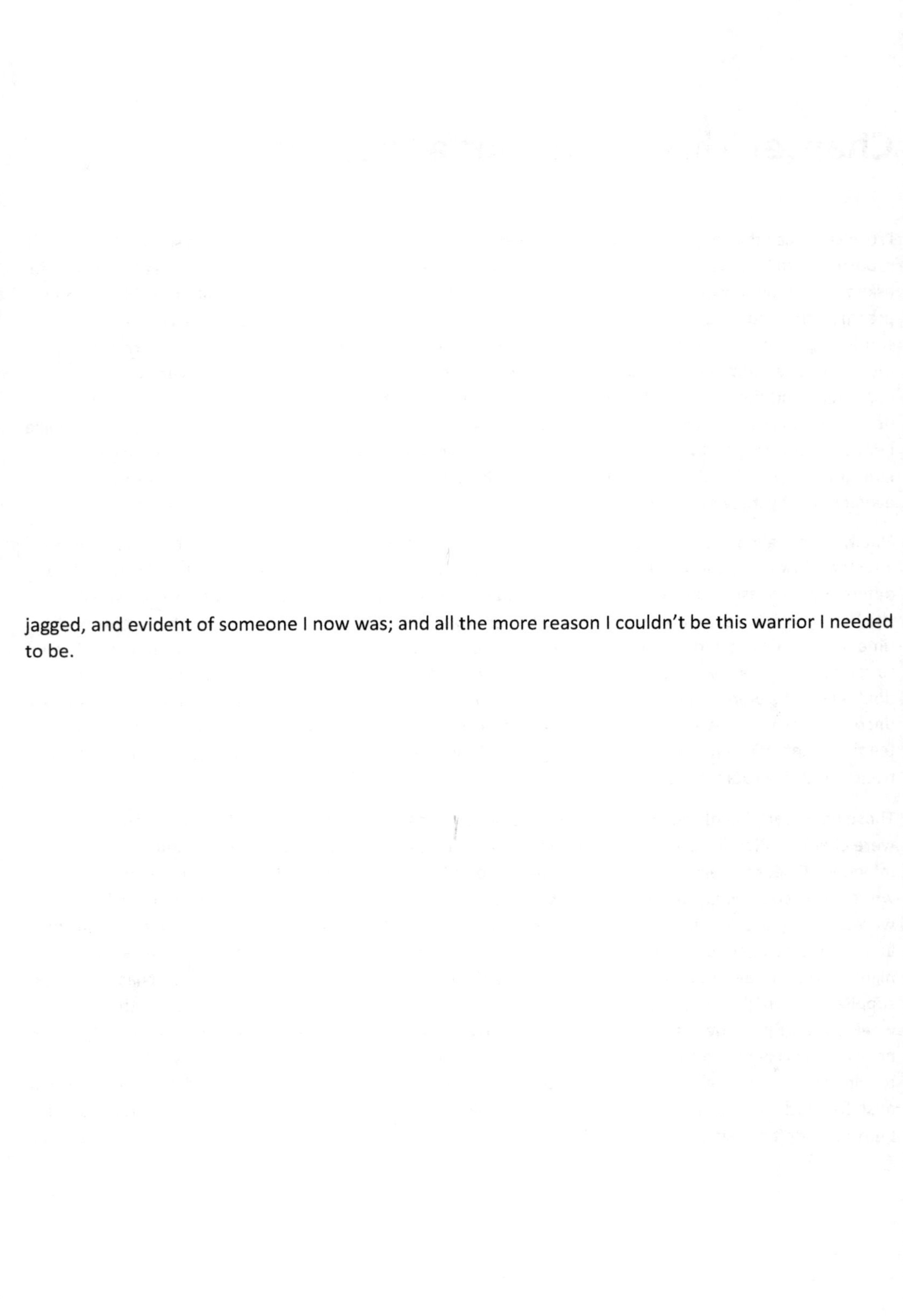

jagged, and evident of someone I now was; and all the more reason I couldn't be this warrior I needed to be.

Chapter Four ~ Where Do I Go from Here?

I concluded September 2019 with a follow-up MRI from surgery and my visit with my neurosurgeon. I can honestly tell you that having the MRI done on a day when he is not in clinic is not recommended and Dr. Google is not your friend. I tossed and turned the days before and up to my follow-up visit. I tortured myself. Yet, I prayed. I was praying. I was reading my Bible. I re-read Psalms. I read about David crying out to God and I knew what that feeling was like. I read on that God brought David out of the cave safely. He was after God's own heart. I wanted to be like David, but where do I go from here?

My MRI results revealed I no longer had a tumor and it indicated Ted the Tumor had been successfully removed. I would report back in a year for a repeat scan. The neurosurgeon said, "You are healed". Thank you, God! I returned for another follow-up with my local doctor, and she moved me from active treatment for the tumor to post-treatment. Sadly, I wasn't joyful. Fear had wrapped itself so much around me that I could not find joy. I wouldn't dare feel something joyful or happy. I would always be prepared for the rug to be pulled out from under me. I would be prepared. I would examine every change my body experienced. I would call about everything I had to make sure there was no sign of infection.

I recall my first sinus infection and the doctor placing me on an antibiotic citing he was concerned it could travel to my brain that we would take all precautions necessary. I never knew that was possible. I worried and constantly checked my temperature. I refused to take Tylenol to ensure I knew whether I had a fever or not. I endured that sinus infection, but the anxiety was far worse. There was nothing like it. I worked with high anxiety and pushed my body through long nights and weekends, even when I really didn't have to do so. I was wearing my body out with it and dragging those that loved me along with me.

I was torn, weary, broken, and bruised. I wanted peace more than anything. I desperately wanted to find the peace I needed to know that I was truly healed. I relied heavily on the book of Psalms and Matthew 6:25-33. However, I could read them a hundred times, but I had to let all of this go and give it to God. I just wasn't ready yet. Not really. I'd give it to Him and take it back. Always keeping the ropes tightly wound around my hands thinking I could control the outcome. I could make it where all of this would not happen again. I could control my body and potential infections around me. I was stealing the very peace I wanted for myself. I simply had to give it to Him, but I was afraid. I was afraid I had disappointed God so much, how could He love me? I had done something wrong to warrant this awful journey. I was talking, but He wasn't hearing me. Or was He?

God was listening, but I was hard-headed. He had been there the entire time, carrying me in the days I felt so defeated, and healing me. He was working on my faith. He was working to show me how to restore it and to find joy in my journey. He had never left, and I was not being punished. He was fulfilling every promise He has ever made. I just needed to be still, give it to the Lord, take his yoke upon me, and I would find the peace I sought.

Chapter Five ~ God, where are you?

The rest of 2019 was filled with perspective. I sought to find myself. I started therapy and tried to work on myself. I sought the peace. I tried to give a little bit more to God each day. I would have to talk myself down from the ledge on the days my anxiety robbed me of my joy. I attended my church and my Mama's church on most Sundays. I soaked up as much as I could learn about the Lord. I needed answers. I needed to know.

I still missed much of the point God was trying to make. Hindsight is 20/20 they say. I entered 2020 working as I had always done. Changes in the behavioral health system were coming and I was going to be ready. I worked long hours still and occasionally some weekends to beat whatever I feared to the punch. I wanted to be prepared. I wanted to excel. I wanted to be the very best. I was going to be the person I had always been. Whatever I looked like in the mirror or had been through, I was going to be her again. I was going to be Crystal. Not this new woman before me. I was going to find my peace in being here. Ladies and gentlemen, that doesn't work either.

In March 2020, our rescue pup I talked Cameron into, Miss Candy Lucy needed my attention and Ashleigh wanted a bath. She never had an issue with hot water. Water temperature was usually too cold, and I wanted her to wait until I came back from keeping Miss Candy from having an accident in the house. When I got back in, it was too late. Ashleigh had climbed into a tub of hot water. She suffered second degree burns and I was home alone. I called Mama and she was not home. Cameron was away and I could not reach him. I drove her to the emergency room, and they immediately took care of her. My stepsister, Amie, happened to be working this day and she was a familiar face that Ashleigh needed. She was sent to UNC – Chapel Hill's burn center. I rode in the ambulance's front seat, while I could see Ashleigh in the back on the gurney. She had already swindled the cell phone of the driver's companion. Another step in my journey, and it was etched with the most horrible failure as a mother I believed. I still wasn't making God happy with me. I prayed over my daughter as the nursing staff washed the silver cream that was previously applied and bandaged her. Ashleigh asked me to come in and they said it would be best if I was there to help her through it. The doctors performed surgery and we spent March through July going through the process of care for burn patients.

All the while, COVID had crept into our world. We were shut down. I began to work from home. The children couldn't go to school. Cameron was the only one working outside of the home. Nickolas and Ashleigh's senior was unprecedented as places closed and we were on a country-wide lockdown. There was no prom and graduation was "drive-up". Thankfully, we saw them both graduate, one behind the other, and my Mama heart was so proud. Nickolas was slated to go to boot camp in August. We decided to take a trip to my cousin, Bobby and Laurie's beach home in Beaufort, NC. Kristin accompanied Nick and Mama came, too. We made the best out of our trip there. We even learned the difference between a cemetery and graveyard. Ask any of us.

August came quickly and it was time for Nickolas to leave for boot camp. Cameron, Gracie, and Kristin rode to Raleigh, along with Nickolas' mom, Beth. We celebrated that day with a home cooked meal. It was truly a Thanksgiving meal with Mama's carrot cake. Friends and family celebrated and the pictures we captured will last a lifetime.

I poured myself into therapy and attending church. I became more comfortable with living more. We took trips on the weekends, always including Kristin. We travelled on day trips to places around North Carolina. We visited historic sites and local places to eat. We fell in love with a Carthage and Sanford, North Carolina eatery. We were on a mission to try something new on those weekend trips.

Unfortunately, COVID got us. Mama called my cell phone. She had moved in with us when Nickolas went to boot camp. She cold barely breathe. I quickly got dressed and drove her to Duke Raleigh. I had to drop her off at the emergency department door. I slept in the Jeep for a few hours, and they released her. She was diagnosed with COVID. Within a day, Cameron and myself had it. Ashleigh and Riley were home and remained secluded to their rooms staying away from us. Family and friends dropped supplies off and God answered my prayers. We were all okay.

Once we were released from quarantine, we resumed traveling about. We made plans for the holidays to visit Nickolas in tech school. Graduation from boot camp was televised. We sent weekly notes and watched online. We waited dearly for our weekly telephone calls. Nickolas called to inform us just before Christmas we would not be able to visit him at the end of December. Secretly, he was planning to surprise us for Christmas. Boy, did he ever! I think the entire neighborhood across the street heard me yell. It is a moment I will treasure always, and so thankful Beth captured it on video. While Nickolas was home, he proposed to Kristin, and we were over the moon. Something was lurking though. There was a red spot on my forehead and a crater had begun. I had it checked out by the urgent care physician's assistant, and he feared that that my bone flap may be infected right after Christmas. He suggested I follow up with my neurosurgeon and local doctor.

I followed up with my local doctor and we tried ointments first. She had performed a lab and there were no signs of infection growing. I shrugged it off. Besides, Nickolas and Kristin had set a date after his graduation from tech school in March. He would come home, marry, and move to South Dakota...All in one week. What a beautiful wedding it was. COVID was still lurking, but we were ready to celebrate. Nickolas had accomplished so much. We were blessed, yet sadden they were moving so far away Nickolas was married on a Thursday, packed on a Friday, and pulled out on a Saturday for South Dakota. The sight of the U-Haul leaving brought us to tears.

I had a dermatologist appointment while Cameron and Mama planned to drive them to South Dakota. The appointment was not what I wanted to hear. The doctor believed it to be a bone flap malfunction possibly due to infection. The infection was tunneling out of my forehead. I was gripped by the same fears from before. I had grown in my faith, but the anxiety I had was so faithful that it knew what to say. The devil is always looking for an opportunity and he found one. I contacted my neurosurgeon, and they asked I come to clinic that same day. I telephoned my stepmom, Gail, and Dad. They took me to Durham and Gail went with me to see the doctor. She accompanied me to the CT scan. I had packed a bag prepared to stay, since I had to with the last infection. My neurosurgeon said it appeared some infection was present and that I would be recommended to a plastic surgeon for consultation. What I dreaded in July 2019 was uttered, bone flap removal for six months followed up by a plate insertion.

I attended my appointment with the plastic surgeon, and he planned to conduct a surgery in tandem with my neurosurgeon to remove my bone flap. I reported for surgery on April 30, 2021. Sixteen days after Riley's fifteenth birthday. Another surgery triggered my children and at this time, they were home schooled. I promised them I would video chat with them once surgery was complete. I wanted to calm their fears. Cameron had to wait in the parking deck until I got to recovery. He wasn't allowed to see me before I left for the procedure. I met a woman in the lobby area, and we began talking. I truly believe the Lord put her in my path to remind me He was there with me. As I lie there waiting for my turn to go back to the OR, I thought of our conversation and the nurse promised to be there with me. She knew it was hard not to have loved ones there during this time of COVID. I listened to my Christian music, and I prayed. I prayed earnestly as they administered the medication into the OR. I awoke from surgery filled with a joyous spirit...my bone flap was saved. I was joyous, praising my God for what He had done. I called everyone professing the blessing God had bestowed. I shouted to the Lord! I told nurses. I told anyone that would listen. God had blessed me! The wonder working power of the Lord had saved my bone flap.

The remainder of 2021 I earnestly made efforts to give it to God, but I couldn't. I still held back a little bit of that burden. I still could not overcome the anxiety. The depression was better. I even stopped my medication, but the outer elements of the world pecked at me. Talons sharp and ready. I struggled with who I was now. I was altered and I didn't know how to embrace her during these moments. Some days, I never thought of it and others, it lingered and ate away at me.

I dived into work more so than ever. I had a need to be the best I could be. Slowly, I realized I was older, I was functioning at a substandard rate than I had before, and I was doing all I could to keep up. The sensation of the hamster on the wheel never seemed to stop. It seemed like the only rest I got was when I had surgery. There were no other pressures on me. This was not like me AT ALL! I was always the go-getter. I was always the one that could keep up and dance steps ahead. I found myself struggling and wondering had this left me impaired? Had I suffered something? Was I ever going to bounce back? God, where are you?

Chapter Six ~ Goodbye Crystal

When you lose someone, grief takes hold. It's a fickle emotion because it encompasses so many emotions. Overwhelming distraught to the point you cannot breathe, take another step, or move forward. It's met with joy for the heavenly transition, a joy that cannot be described, but yelling a Hallelujah! It's anger because something is missing and there simply was not enough time. It is the weight of handling every single thing before you and feeling like you cannot let anyone down. You must do what is before you. It is the loss that breaks the heart and burdens the soul. It is five letters that seem to crush the human heart. It beckons your spirit downward. Spiraling and out of control. It draws your breathe like it's going to be the last one and your heart beats violently in your chest as you try to catch that next breathe. Those tears. They well up from an ocean within.

I lost part of myself in this journey. I lost the part of me that was feminine. I lost the long, beautiful, hair to a scar riddled scalp. Seemingly torn by the scalpel time and time again. I lost the features of my face that made me whole. It was riddled with craters and deformities where I couldn't look at my own husband and feel the beauty he saw. It was the shaved head and donning various coverings for people to stare with empathetic glimpses or awkwardly trying to figure out just what was going on. I never considered myself a beautiful, knock-out, drop dead gorgeous woman, but I was comfortable in who I was.

It was the soul shattering loss of the person I was. She died when Ted was found. The confident woman who prided herself on being the overachiever and needing to control her life. I wanted to live a life where I made the rules and handled the pressure. I wanted it one way and that was my way. I wanted to work and be number one at anything I did because I thought that was expected of me. I lived behind a life of high functioning anxiety and the shell of a Christian. I believed in God whole heartedly, but I didn't know how to live for God, to trust in His timing, and to give Him my life. How ironic because I never had control of anything. The very things I needed and yearned for most of my life were exactly what God had promised to give me. I wouldn't commit.

God committed himself to me more than 2000 years ago. He had committed to me before I was formed. He was committed to the Crystal he wanted me to become. He brought me on this journey to lose the old Crystal. He wanted me to be born again. I had to plant my mustard seeds firmly in soil that I nurtured and not between a rocky and sandy soil. It would never take root properly and it would die. He had the very blessings I needed and desired to bestow them upon me, but first I needed to learn. I needed to grieve the Crystal I was and embrace the new woman of faith he wanted me to become. I still stumble along the way, but I earnestly try to follow the mapped out steps God has for me. My goal is to seek Him. Again, I fall short. Sin is very real and the devil is here to lie, cheat, and destroy. I have worked on trying to recognize the traps the devil has for me.

I grieved for the Crystal before Ted the Tumor and grieve for her still, but I cannot stay in my grief because the Lord has prepared something far greater.

Chapter Seven ~ God's Plan

From September through December 2021, we endured a near loss. Cameron's mother had a "widow maker" heart attack. Cameron aided his stepfather in caring for his mother in the hospital and later discharge. We brought her home, after a two-day stint at the local rehab. That's another story for another time. We rallied and helped nurse her back to reunite with her husband at home. I worked my social worker magic and linked her with providers and set up a notebook to track her vitals daily. During this another spot arose on my forehead and began to drain. I couldn't deny it was just like the first one that appeared the previous year.

I contacted my plastic surgeon and after a detailed CT scan learned the bone flap had failed. It was necrotic from infection and was dying. The infection was tunneling out of my forehead. I didn't know at the time, but this was a blessing. It never reached my brain. The challenges I was feeling about myself were a direct result of my body fighting an infection. My plastic surgeon scheduled surgery for March 29, 2022. They would contact neurosurgery if the bone flap had to come out and we would plan on a titanium plate six months later.

I decided I would take time off to prepare for this surgery. I was afraid, but I knew that I would be ok. God would see me through it, right?! The day of the surgery, I met with the medical team and was prepped with IVs. I was wheeled into the OR, and I woke up in recovery. Sadly, the neurosurgeon on call would not be able to remove my bone flap that day. It required the skill of my regular neurosurgeon. Cultures were taken and again pseudomonas was the culprit. They found the bone flap had indeed failed and was porous. My bone was dying. It had lost blood supply due to the bone infection. As the neurosurgeon told me I would have to come back for surgery, I wept. Defeated. He held my hand, and they prepared me for discharge. I came home and the worry opened like Pandora's box. I paced and worried about when I would have to do this. I just kept repeating "I need time". I needed time to catch my breath. I needed time to process this all again. I needed time to accept I would be without a bone flap (forehead) for six months. What did this mean? What would I look like? All those familiar haunting feelings ramped up. Finally, I received a call, and my surgery was scheduled for April 19, 2022.

Nickolas and Kristin were visiting from South Dakota. Nickolas had stopped by on the evening of April 17, 2022. We had previously celebrated Riley turning sixteen. I had made sure we went to DMV to obtain his license. I was off the next day for pre-op and the phone rang. It was Duke. It was almost 11:00 p.m. and they were calling. I couldn't imagine why. They called to request I come the next day to undergo the surgery. I agreed. I immediately packed a bag and tried my hardest to get sleep. I had to endure pre-op labs and have surgery in the same day. My anxiety was through the roof. It was finally happening.

I arose the next morning, full of angst, and I packed my Bible. I reported to the surgical waiting room and began to read. I read the words and soaked them in the best I could. I even saw a woman from church.

We spoke words of encouragement and parted ways. The nursing staff called me back, leaving Cameron in the waiting room. I endured a COVID test, labs, IVs (my veins had become horrible to find), visits from the neurosurgeon, and a vast array of other medical professionals. Finally, Cameron was allowed to come back. The hours tarried on as my case was bumped and we waited on the OR. It was getting late. Finally, they took me back. I kissed Cameron and let the tears fall. He squeezed my hand and they wheeled me away.

In the OR room, they talked to me and transitioned me from one gurney to another. I prayed as they had me count down. Several hours later, my bone flap was removed. I awoke in the OR as I was waiting for a bed in recovery. The anxiety swept over me. I was hot again even though I was in a room as cold as an icebox. I felt nauseous. I was ready to be out of there. Once available, I was taken to the recovery area, where Cameron finally joined me. I was so incredibly hot. I felt like I had been dipped in the boughs of Hell and left with a fiery imprint. I couldn't get cool. My anxiety was at an all time high. I felt panicked. The same panicked feeling on that fateful day in May 2019 where the medication had altered my ability to calm. Cameron fanned me with a folded sheet. He did all he could to calm me and fan me. The nurse ended up giving me a PRN medication, but to no avail.

I entered my room in the Neuro-ICU feeling like I would never quench the fire that plagued me. The hotter I was the more my anxiety inched higher. The nurse turned the thermostat down, put ice packs under my arm pits, and left the sheet off me. It took, what seemed like forever, to get me to cool off. It by far has been one of the worst experiences to date. Once I was able to relax, I drifted off to sleep, awakened every so often for vital checks.

The neuro team came by to evaluate me daily. I walked up and down the hallways in hopes I could return home soon. I was ready to go. The drain in my head was removed and the bandages simplified for easier care at home. (Thank goodness for Mama, those bandages stuck to even the shortest hairs on my head. Like the prior year, I had cut it short for easier management.) I was discharged after a few days, with instructions to return in two weeks to remove the stitches in my forehead from the draining areas and three weeks for the scalp stitches.

Cameron and I traveled back to Durham to be fitted for my prosthetic helmet. I can honestly say, I was not looking forward to it. I tried to put on a brave face because I couldn't let my anxiety or depression be known. Cameron and Mama had endured so much dealing with it the first go round. Yet, I feared the unknown and my relationship with God seemed to be void of something. I couldn't place it yet, but I missed something. I missed something I frantically needed, but what was it? I attempted to wear the helmet under my hat, but it was so tight. I despised everything it represented. All of it. It was a stumbling block in my journey, and I just wanted it gone. I later learned how valuable it would become.

At the appointed times, I had my stitches removed. The last appointment were the stitches around my scar. There were more than fifty and individually stitched. Two nurses worked on my head for almost two hours, with the neurosurgeon removing a few that were problematic. The nurses took breaks, offering me breaks throughout the way, but they had grown weary from it. I had not. I recited 2 Timothy 1:7. God was going to handle this battle. I was going to make it through. After the most tedious session of stitch removal to date, I left the office feeling the power of the Almighty God.

I had realized in the first few weeks of my recovery; I could not go through it with the rousing feelings of depression. I would NOT let the devil win. God sent blessings in the friends and family to encourage my spirit. My cousin, Amber, and I conversed and by the end of the call, I contacted my local doctor and therapist for help. I also realized how important it was to get to know God. I knew God, but I didn't know his Word. I knew what I had heard in sermons, Sunday school, inspirational books, etc. I announced to my Mama I was going to read the Bible, from cover to cover, and get to know God. I was going to read it before my next scheduled surgery in six months. I yearned to know God's Word for me. I wanted to see what it said, envelope it within my spirit, and etch it upon my soul. I set out each day reading. I would read at night before bed, and I grew my spirit. I listened to songs and read. I highlighted passages where God promised healing. I understood I was not being punished. I had a spirit not of fear, but one of power, love, and self-control (2 Timothy 1:7). I became closer with God through my relationship with Jesus. Glory! Hallelujah!

I prepared for my annual scan at the end of the September 2022. Cameron took off work to accompany me. I was able to enter the MRI without angst, even though I had some medication to help me out. The nurse inserted the IV for contrast while the other held me hand. My headphones were placed on my head, and I listened to the sounds of praise music. I prayed in that machine that the results would be favored if it was God's will. Cameron and I left the Duke Mobile Unit headed for Durham. We met with my neurosurgeon and learned my tumor had not grown, but one had formed over my left orbit. I was shocked. It would be removed at my next surgery. I wanted to know why, but God said it wasn't for me to know right now. I recognized the tumor did not grow. God had answered my prayers. He had heard the prayers of everyone. I left there and consulted with my new plastic surgeon. He explained how the titanium plate would be affixed to my skull and discussed recovery based on his interventions. I would need a new CT scan and the measurements would be sent off. The plate would return in two to three weeks and surgery would be scheduled with both doctors completing their respective procedures. It was a lot of information to absorb. I left there with Cameron, and we finished our afternoon delighting in each other's presence. We were not going to let the devil ruin our day.

The following week, I reported to Duke Raleigh for my CT scan. It took a few minutes to be administered and I was on my way. I waited longer in the waiting room due to an updated ordered needed. Cameron and I went to the mall, ate lunch, and walked around. We had a high school reunion to attend the weekend. Cameron selected a dress and shoes that he thought would be ideal. I realized I had to find the joy in my journey...PERMANENTLY. I had to really give it to God. I had to seek Him above all else. I attended my twenty-fifth reunion and absolutely had a blast. I made the little moments count. I couldn't take pictures because I was too busy making memories. Thank God for the fellowship with folks I haven't seen in a while. Most importantly, I was blessed to be comfortable in my own skin and how good the new Crystal looked. It wasn't about my outside features, but the way I felt on the inside. The damage the devil tried to do; God undid.

Chapter Eight ~ The Never-Ending, Never-Failing Love of God

I read and pray seeking answers to things the devil had planted in my head for so long. I rebuked them. I felt my anxiety and depression fall from my spirit even as badly as the devil wanted it to stay in the days that have passed. I rebuked the devil at the calling of Jesus' name. I have prayed in the morning, during the day, and even in the middle of the night, God will restore my health. I pray for others. I continuously pray. I cry, but not out of sorrow. I cry tears of joy. I let go of the picture of who I thought I was supposed to be, the Crystal prior to all of this, and embrace the one that depicts the steps of this journey.

Along the way, God has positioned people, events, and situations in my life to bring about my growth in faith, submission to His Word, and hope. My cousin allowed God to write her story of breast cancer. It was a journey I didn't know the intimate details, but I connected in our similar struggles of scanxiety (the sheer anxiety that arises when you have a scan of any kind); disappointments when the news is not what we want to hear, rather trusting in God's timing; struggling to find the joy when the journey wears you out; and testifying to God's Word. We reached out to each other and encouraged each other. Amid her own journey, she took the time to pray for me and call on her own prayer warriors to do the same. I alike did the same. I watched a story unfold as God penned the pages of her life detailing great faith, spiritual strength, and a testimony of God's presence in her life. While her last earthly breath was drawn in August 2022, her story is ongoing. It's ongoing in the impact her testimony made in the lives of others, especially mine. She was God's blessing to me. She was undoubtedly the person I needed to conquer the next steps of my own journey through her testimony.

Along the journey, friends and family have matched my steps along the way. They have come to my house and watched movies with me; opened their hearts to listen to my anxiety or depression and offered me their enduring love and prayers; and taken me for rides throughout the country when I couldn't be in public. They have fed us countless meals and helped us with our children. Never asking for anything in return, they have given themselves much like Christ did. They have let us lean on them, even when I worried if the weight of it all was too much. I recall a weekday excursion with my Mama's sister, Selma, cousin Faye, and Mama. We traveled to an eatery and spent much of the day riding here and there. We wound up at Aunt Thelma's house, Selma's twin sister, to visit. We chatted and ended our day. The one thing I recall was Mama telling me how much those three ladies prayed for me. They called to check on me during their weekly, if not daily, phone calls. Something as simple as a day galivanting repaid the prayers whispered over me.

I have leaned into prayer and prayed for myself. This was something I didn't think I could do. I have requested prayer from others. My name has been added to prayer lists in churches where people I don't know pray for me. They speak words of their faith over my name. I have been anointed before surgeries and doctor's appointments. I have seen the power of God's assembly lay hands upon me and come together to pray for my healing. I have learned of family standing in my place to receive anointed healing on my behalf. I have kneeled on an old fashioned alter and laid it there asking Jesus to take my burdens from me and restore my health to turn to find my Mama alongside me letting me turn inward to her as God bottles up the tears I shed. I have been to the alter with my children, Ashleigh and Riley, and watched as my children prayed for their Mama as I clutch them and pray for God not to take me from them. I have asked for forgiveness as I tarry this road because I am a sinner saved by the grace of God. I am not perfect, but I seek perfection in Christ, and even though I still fail Him; He still seeks me from the ninety-nine.

Chapter Nine ~ Chronicles of a Brain Tumor Warrior

I didn't know it then, but in 2019 I began blogging my journey. Each step on my personal Facebook page, and now later my Chronicles of a Brain Tumor Warrior- Crystal's Journey Facebook page. I have chronicled the steps of this journey through the present. I know there are more steps to conquer, but I will not be shaken. God Almighty has brought me further in my faith giving me the very things I have yearned for all my life. This journey was not about the tumor, but about God's testament of his glory and grace. I cannot give credit to anyone for saving my life, but Jesus Christ. That cross bears every sin I have committed, and the commitment God has to me. I am not worthy, but He believes I am.

Asking for prayers.
I have learned some medical news today, but still need more answers. ♥
Brain Tumor Warrior- Crystal's Journey

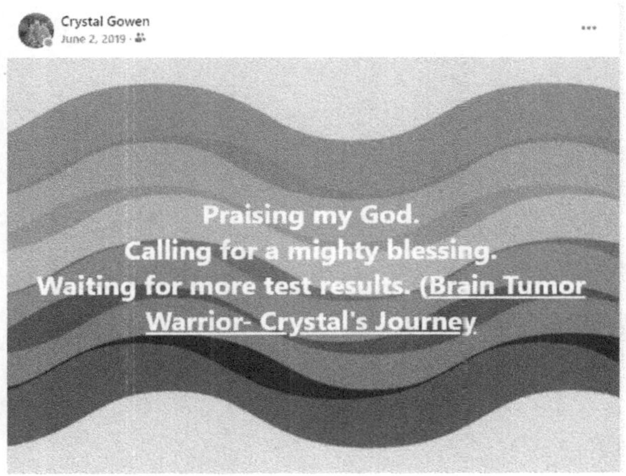

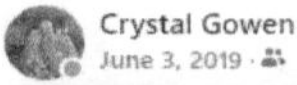

Appointment tomorrow.
Praying for good results.
Thank you all for your texts, messages, and calls.

Crystal Gowen shared a memory.
June 4, 2019 ·

In my darkest days..
Even when I thought I was at the bottom...
He never faltered..
I was always told the silver linings in clouds were Hope....
More than ever I believe it today.
(Brain Tumor Warrior- Crystal's Journey

5 Years Ago
See your memories >

Focus on the Family
May 28, 2017 ·

"For I am sure that neither death nor life, nor angels nor rulers, nor things present nor things to come, nor powers, nor height nor depth, nor anything else in all creation, will be able to separate us from the love of God in Christ Jesus our Lord." Romans 8:38-39

If you are breathing,
there is
Hope.
God
can reach farther
than you can fall.
Dennis Jernigan

Crystal Gowen
June 4, 2019 ·

As I reflect today, I'm grateful for the power of prayer. From prayer chains to prayer lists, I'm in awe of the love that surrounds me. I received texts of prayers in the midst of my doctor's appointment reminding me to claim the blessings and protection of God Almighty. Two women, near and dear to my heart, placed by God in a waiting room bringing forth peace to me, not even knowing my situation. Helping me battle nerves the devil charged against me. The news we received today was not the worst because it was filled with hope. I have a tumor (non-cancerous) in the middle of my brain. I don't have a symptom in the world. An unlucky fall after the Paul McCartney concert resulted in a precautionary CT and subsequent MRI scan which brought us to finding this slow growing mass. As a wonderful friend told me recently if God brings you to it, He will see you through it. When my mustard seed of faith seemed faint, He sent in warriors with messages, phone calls, texts, and love.

A husband that I love more than anything for being my rock, keeping me laughing, and being there every step of the way. Letting me cry, worry, and even take us away for a day. He has sat in the MRI room with me and watched over me. He has been my biggest supporter. My Mama who has kept watch as if I was a baby. Age doesn't matter at all. She has motivated me to have faith, even in my despair of the unknown. My Dad and Gail for keeping me positive and watching the kids. My sister for keeping me focused and letting me say I'm scared when I needed to. My Aunt Pam and Uncle Tommy keeping up with me, even during their vacation, and for exhaling. I think we did it at the same time.❤ For my friends and extended family praying over me, claiming blessings, and healing. For my EP family and their support today. My church family and Pastor's messages. I love you all.

My journey has just begun. We are working toward treatment to rid my brain of this tumor. It cannot live any longer as the status quo or my own quality of life will be negatively impacted. Boot straps up because I got grit, which makes this pearl shine. More appointments to follow and more decisions to be made I'm sure. Thank you all for your prayers and for loving me.
Brain Tumor Warrior- Crystal's Journey

Crystal Gowen
June 8, 2019 ·

Lord, I'm praying.
I'm trying to worry less, but Anxiety Girl (my alter ego) could be fitted for a super hero costume with a cape and all. I'm praying to worry less, praying for a successful surgery (date TBD), and I'm praying for my husband, children, and those who love me to get through this with during my recovery.

Crystal Gowen
June 11, 2019 ·

You never know what can happen in life. I was just at a concert and took a fall. The fall was caused by a spilled beverage on concrete steps. I didn't expect to be faced with a brain tumor (olfactory meniginoma- typically the largest intracranial brain tumor) before my 40th birthday approaches. Here I am... I'm facing a tumor about 4 cm and we've named him Ted. Mostly to provide some humor to our situation and to keep us all sane. Today, my surgeon at Duke has decided to give Ted his eviction notice on June 20th. I will go June 19th for pre-op and be admitted. Ted can't live here any longer. He's simply too big and while I've not had a symptom yet, I don't want any. God has brought me here and I've struggled. I've struggled with faith and trying to keep my anxiety at bay. I've struggled with feeling like I should have more faith than I do. I've struggled with the overwhelming sensation of how quickly this has happened. I've shed tears, paced, and been fearful. Yet my testimony is this...God has not forsaken me. He's brought forth witnesses to remind me I am a child of God and to profess my faith, and it is not a lost faith. Why?! Because my God knew even before I did what I would need. Continue to pray for my husband, kids, and family. Pray for my team at Duke. Pray for me. #evictted Brain Tumor Warrior- Crystal's Journey

Crystal Gowen
June 16, 2019 ·

Today has been the epitome of family. Celebrating Father's Day and Gracie's birthday are God's blessings in my life. Of course, Ted came up in conversation, but that's where my testimony begins. The circle of people among me today to share in my blessings radiate the reminder of God's love and support of me. A reminder that the beauty in the blessings cannot be overshadowed by Ted and once he's gone, the rejoicing we will do. God said we would be faced with troubles like a mother who experiences the pain of childbirth, but it would be overcome by the sheer joy of the babe she brings into this world.

So Ted.....

Na Na Na Na...Hey..hey...hey...goodbye!

You will not block the work my God has planned for me to do. #evictTed

Brain Tumor Warrior- Crystal's Journey

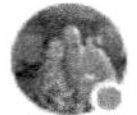

Crystal Gowen is with Connie Ballance.
June 17, 2019 ·

Isaiah 54:17
New International Version
no weapon forged against you will prevail, and you will refute every tongue that accuses you. This is the heritage of the servants of the LORD, and this is their vindication from me," declares the LORD.

Thank you Mrs. Margaret for this verse today. My sleep was poor and the devil was busy. Rebuke him in Jesus name.

Brain Tumor Warrior- Crystal's Journey

Crystal Gowen
June 18, 2019 ·

O, how He loves us...
He will shine his love through the very people in our lives.
Just this evening, my dearest friend sent me a text to say she was thinking of me and she has begun wearing our high school class ring as a reminder to keep me in prayer. My cousin has poured her heart out sharing her own disdain as I go through evicting Ted. I believe my God will see me through this ordeal for the sheer love He has shown me. O, how He loves us. Brain Tumor Warrior- Crystal's Journey

YOUTUBE.COM
Passion - How He Loves (Live) ft. Crowder
Official live video for "How He Loves" from Passion 2015Get Passion's Latest Album "Follow Yo...

Crystal Gowen
June 19, 2019 ·

I am a mountain mover, water walker
More than just an overcomer
'Cause I've been set free
I am a gospel preacher, heart on fire
Freedom singing, testifier
'Cause I've been redeemed
I am a believer
I am a believer

As we travel and the miles pass by, we forge onward to Duke.

We are sealing each page with words that praise our God because we are believers. We have had hands laid upon us; prayed over for healing, strength, recovery, and continued faith from every person we encounter through this chapter; and annoited today. What a beautiful experience to share with my husband. I have hugged my children tightly and shared cuddles with my youngest son because he asked. I've promised them hugs upon my return and their beautiful hearts plan to help Mom. These pages are inked with the power of prayer, fasting (thank you Mrs. Margaret), love, faith, and hope. Even as I clutch to my mustard seed, I pray for each of them as they tarry this road with me.

The Lord our Savior has provided love to me in each of you. The magnitude of this gift is far beyond what I could have imagined.

Brain Tumor Warrior- Crystal's Journey

YOUTUBE.COM
Rhett Walker - Believer (Official Lyric Video)

Crystal Gowen
June 19, 2019 ·

I have be been admitted. I'm on the Neuroscience floor for tonight. Surgery tomorrow at noonish. I'll be in ICU tomorrow. Keeping my anxiety at bay, but it wavers. Thank you all for your concerns and texts. I'm ready to evict Ted and turn the page to another chapter. Keeping my mustard seed tightly within my grasp. GPS MRI next and lots of monitoring.

Crystal Gowen
June 20, 2019 ·

Matthew 17:20, Jesus said, "Because you have so little faith. Truly I tell you, if you have faith like a grain of mustard seed, you can say to this mountain, 'Move from here to there,' and it will move.

I have to hold steadfast in my faith. God knows I'm scared, yet he wraps his love around me. I feel it from every person I hear from and those I am not aware saying prayers, fasting, sharing my story, etc. It's time to hold this mustard seed and tell the devil my God has got me.

Ted,

You may not be an actual mountain, but you have to move from here. Eviction is at noon. Please leave kindly as I've provided hospitality the past six years. Leave me with some sort of sense of smell, back away from my sinuses, leave my nerves alone near my eyes, and most importantly try to leave me as you found me. I considered myself in great condition when you moved in and I expect at least mint condition. I'm sure you'll leave a mess, but I'll waive your deposit fee. Just leave. See Ted, I have a mustard seed and I'm not afraid to use it. It's faith and Jesus Christ my Lord and Savior already knows the plans God has made for me. While you were part of the plan, you're not the plan. You're my trouble, my trial, and tribulation. However, there's joy to be had and unfortunately there's no place for you on it.

In Christ's Name

Brain Tumor Warrior- Crystal's Journey

Crystal Gowen
June 20, 2019 ·

Hmmm....
This could be a new Ted look. I'll need an updated dye job tho.
#tedstyles #findthehumor
Brain Tumor Warrior- Crystal's Journey

Crystal Gowen
June 20, 2019 ·

Hey all it's Cameron ! Dr said that her surgery went great and as planned ! Just have to wait to see about her sense of smell . Ted was in there deep but is now evicted !! Thanks to all for the prayers and concerns for the past few days !! Now just to heal from this and keep up the great news !!

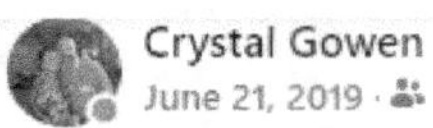

Crystal Gowen
June 21, 2019 ·

I serve the most amazing Lord and Savior!!! Jesus Christ. I made it!! Thank you for the mighty prayer warriors, the staff at Duke especially Dr. Friedman and his team, and the love and support of each of you!! Ted is evicted!!! Here's to recovery!! A new chapter to tell my story. ✝ Brain Tumor Warrior- Crystal's Journey

Crystal Gowen
June 24, 2019 ·

The campaign to #evictted has been successful. However, my testimony doesn't end there. I'm recovering at home with the love and support of family and friends. Prayer works people. God is my great Healer, my Redeemer, and my Savior. May you each know of his everlasting love.

"I am glad I have learned of her meekness
I am proud that my name is on her book
For I want to be one never fearing
The face of my Savior to look.
When He cometh descending from heaven
On the cloud that He writes in His Word
I'll be joyfully carried to meet Him
On the wings of that great speckled bird." - Roy Acuff

Brain Tumor Warrior- Crystal's Journey

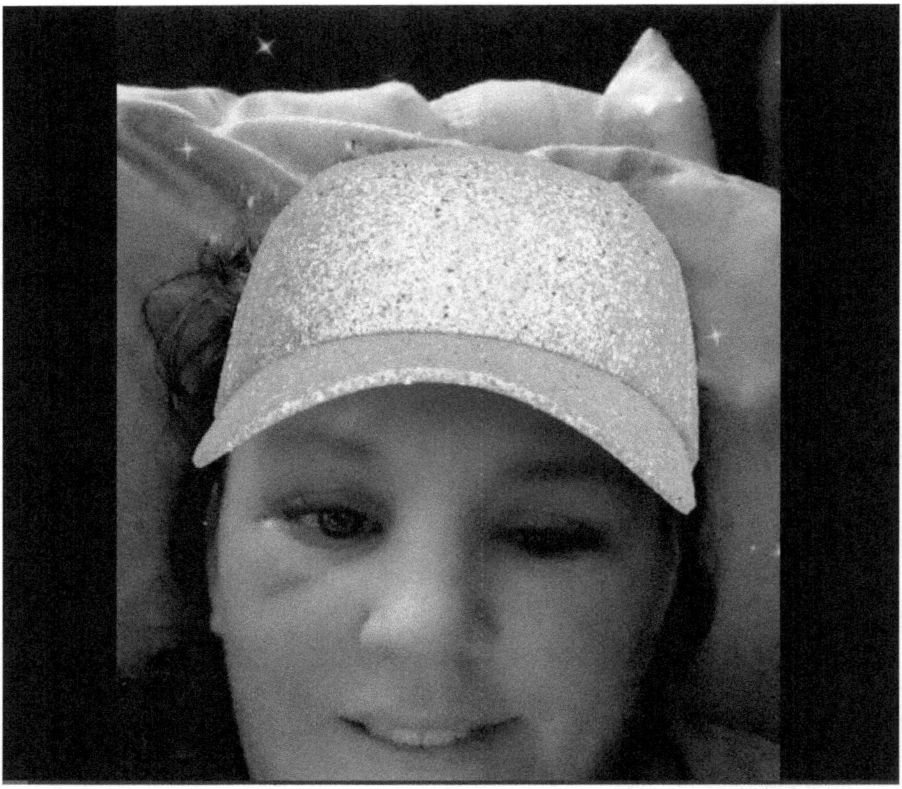

Crystal Gowen
June 25, 2019 · YouTube ·

In a matter of days, I had a whirlwind diagnosis of a brain tumor and surgery to remove Ted (the tumor). Spiritually, God has been working on me and it has taken me time to listen. I was dismayed by my diagnosis and lost my mustard seed along the way. I had to find it, hold strong to it, and keep the faith. I was full of fear: grief, and sadness. The devil tried his best to keep me off course. He wanted me to think God was done. I was in a dark place, planning a funeral my God had no part, and not planting my mustard seed. My family and friends knew God is unfinished with me. It wasn't my time. He has plans for me....
To plant my mustard seed of faith.

My life has changed. I don't know the outcome, but I'm here Lord for you to use me.
Brain Tumor Warrior- Crystal's Journey

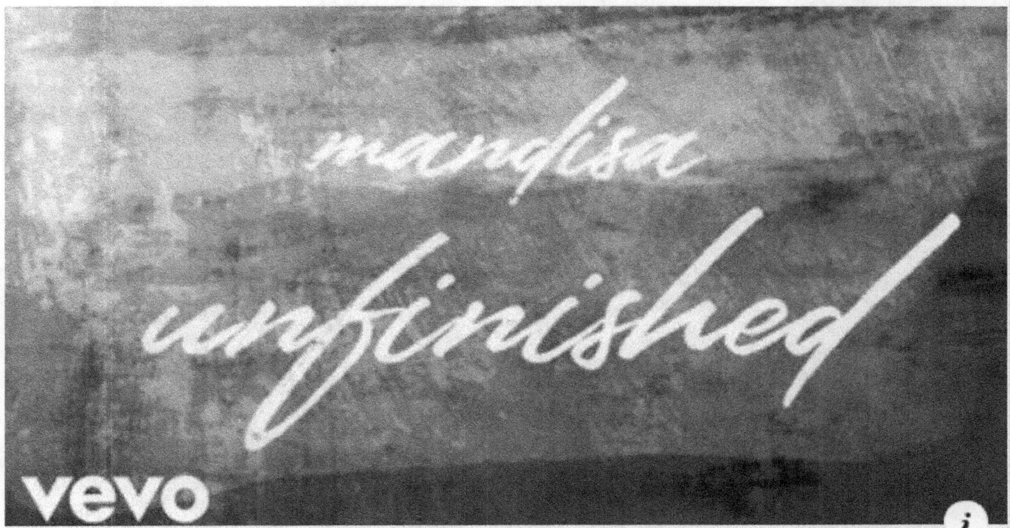

YOUTUBE.COM

Mandisa - Unfinished (Lyric Video)

"Unfinished" (Official Lyric Video) Get this song now on Mandisa's "Overcomer: The Greatest H...

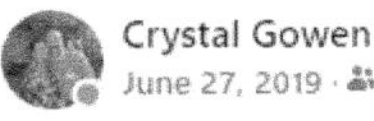

Crystal Gowen
June 27, 2019 ·

Day 7: Seven days since Ted's eviction! Staples to come out Monday! My strength coming back each day! Shout to the Lord! I survived a grade 1 meniginoma brain tumor! Praying steadfast it never returns and my faith never falters! God is good! He's my Great Physician, Healer, Redeemer, and Savior. Thank you for the prayers, texts, calls, and supper! Thank you for letting me share my testimony. I'm saved by His Amazing Grace! Brain Tumor Warrior- Crystal's Journey

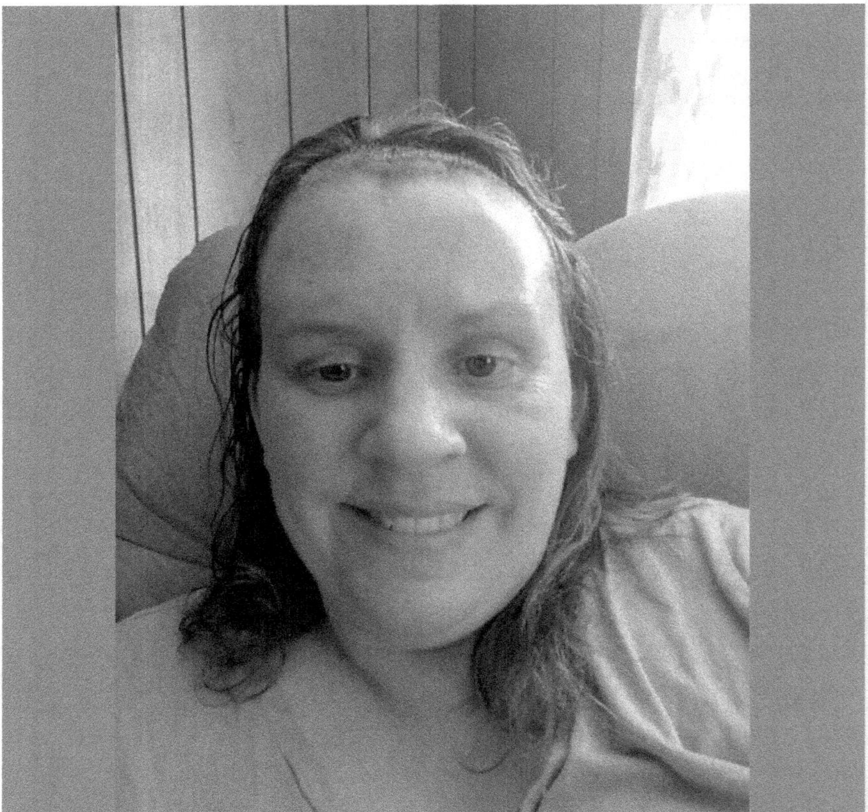

Crystal Gowen
June 28, 2019 ·

I don't know why Ted is part of my story. I laid awake in the wee hours of the morning pondering it. It made me think of Kris Kristofferson's song "Why me Lord?" What did I do that made you want me to share my journey? I have family and friends who have tarried harder roads, face(d) uncertainties, and continue to do so every day. Don't get my wrong....I am grateful for my life, my Lord, and my ever renewed faith. Scattering those mustard seeds in my garden, letting the very people of my life bless them and nourish them, and holding steadfast into the promises. Brain Tumor Warrior- Crystal's Journey

I do not believe the Lord pours heartache into our lives.

I don't know why He allows it in.

But I know that God can use it when it comes.

I know our pain is not pointless.

I've seen that it's actually through our suffering that we can know Christ on a deeper level.

And I know that He uses these times to show us His faithfulness...

Kelli Bachara,
The Unraveling Blog

Because it's right there in the brokennness that He shows us we were never meant to do this on our own, anyway.

Crystal Gowen
June 28, 2019 ·

Why me Lord, what have I ever done
To deserve even one
Of the pleasures I've known
Tell me Lord, what did I ever do
That was worth loving you
Or the kindness you've shown.
Lord help me Jesus, I've wasted it so
Help me Jesus I know what I am
Now that I know that I've need you so
Help me Jesus, my soul's in your hand.
Tell me Lord, if you think there's a way
I can try to repay
All I've taken from you
Maybe Lord, I can show someone else
What I've been through myself
On my way back to you.
Lord help me Jesus, I've wasted it so
Help me Jesus I know what I am
Now that I know that I've need you so
Help me Jesus, my soul's in your hand.
"Why Me Lord"

Crystal Gowen
June 29, 2019 ·

God is amazing! Keeping my spirits up as best as I can. The hubby and kids want to get out today. Wish us luck. Trying a beautiful hair wrap, even with staples, to cover this dome of mine. Thank you all for everything! Love is beautiful. A true gift from above. Please join us next month to celebrate my recovery journey. Brain Tumor Warrior- Crystal's Journey

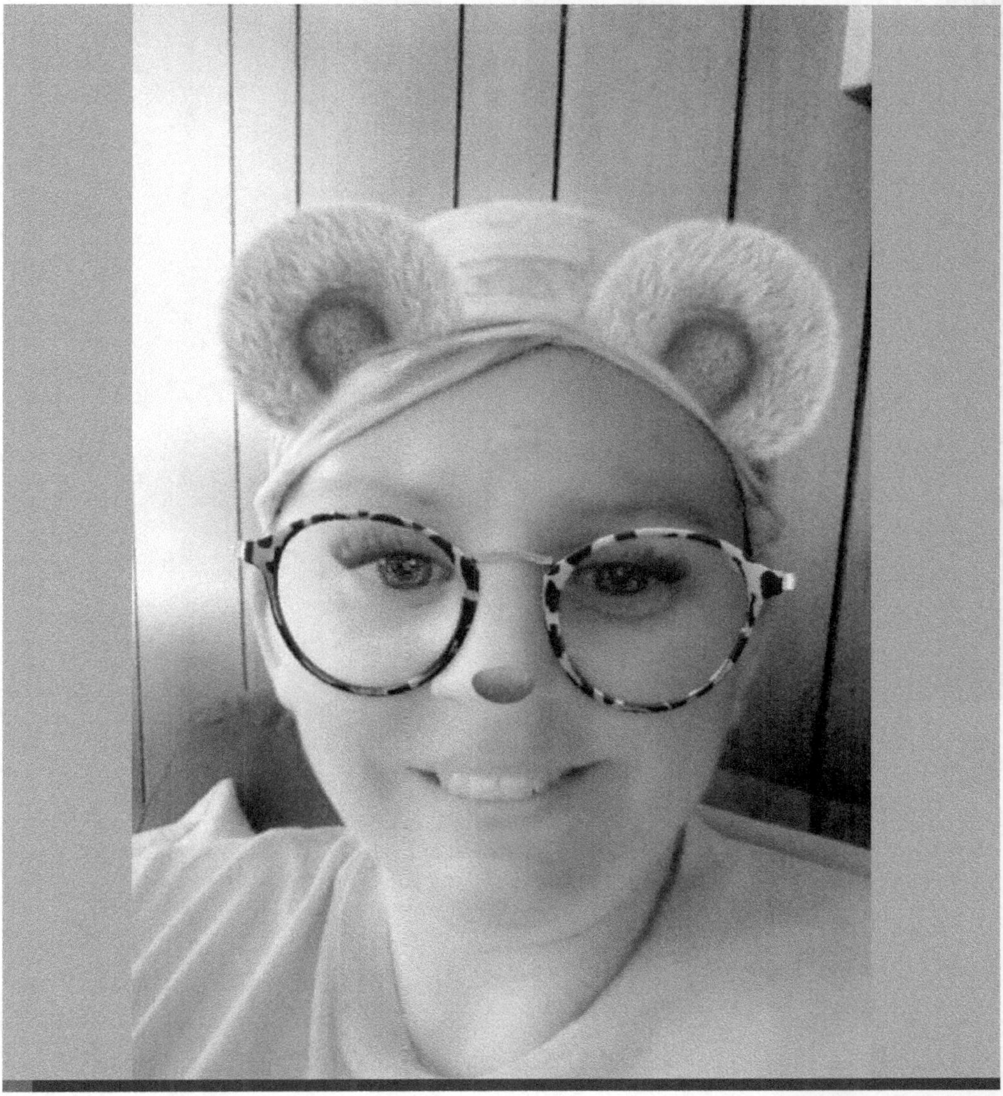

Crystal Gowen
July 1, 2019 ·

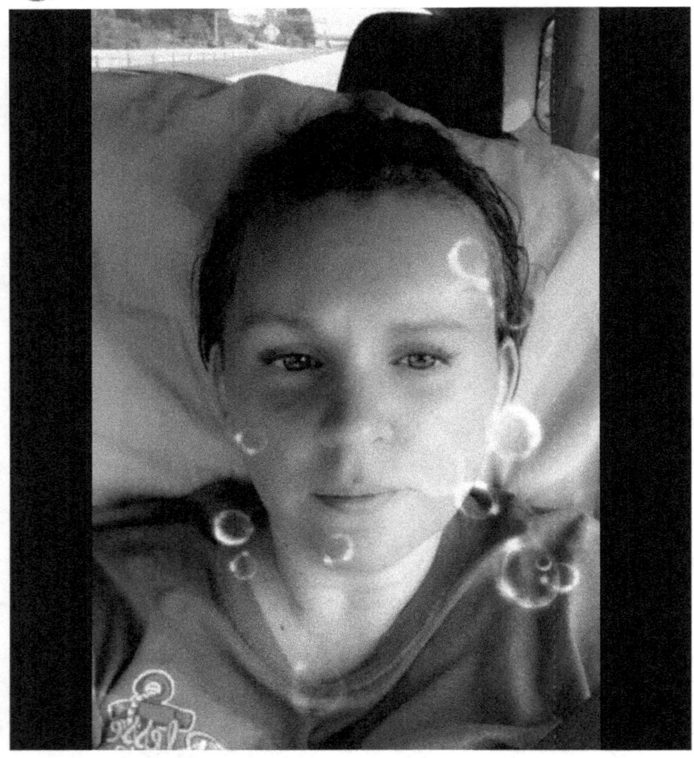

Crystal Gowen
July 2, 2019 ·

Lord,
I praise you for bringing me through. I pray for comfort and healing. Take away the ache and bless me with sleep. Let tomorrow dawn with better spirits and you in my focus.

Amen

Crystal Gowen
July 5, 2019 ·

15 days post brain surgery.
I've got some fuzz growing back at my incision site.
All incisions are healing well- head, lumbar drain, and stomach to repair my sinuses.
I'm thankful y'all! My life has been saved in more ways than one! Brain Tumor Warrior- Crystal's Journey

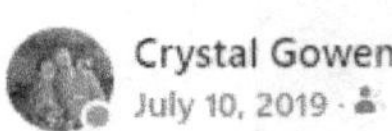

Crystal Gowen
July 10, 2019 ·

I have to give a huge shout out to my husband, Cameron Gowen. Y'all when he brought me home twenty days ago, he slept in the den either in the recliner, love seat, or air mattress. He never left my side. He set alarms for around the clock medication passes. Now, he's gone back to work all the while taking care of the house, me, and our babies. He's an amazing husband and partner in life's journey. I'm extremely grateful God has given me a wonderful husband. Brain Tumor Warrior- Crystal's Journey

Crystal Gowen is with **Brandie Black** and **6 others**.
July 11, 2019 ·

Three weeks ago I wasn't sure if God had a plan for me to witness this moment, but I give God all the glory to witness it and for Nickolas' decision to serve our great nation and stake his life on the principles this nation was founded. Half the room was filled with the family who loves him greatly and I'm super happy to be a part of it. We are so proud of you!! You're officially sworn in and we are Air Force proud!!! #blendedfamilieswork #airforceproud #theygrowupfast Brain Tumor Warrior- Crystal's Journey

Crystal Gowen
July 14, 2019 ·

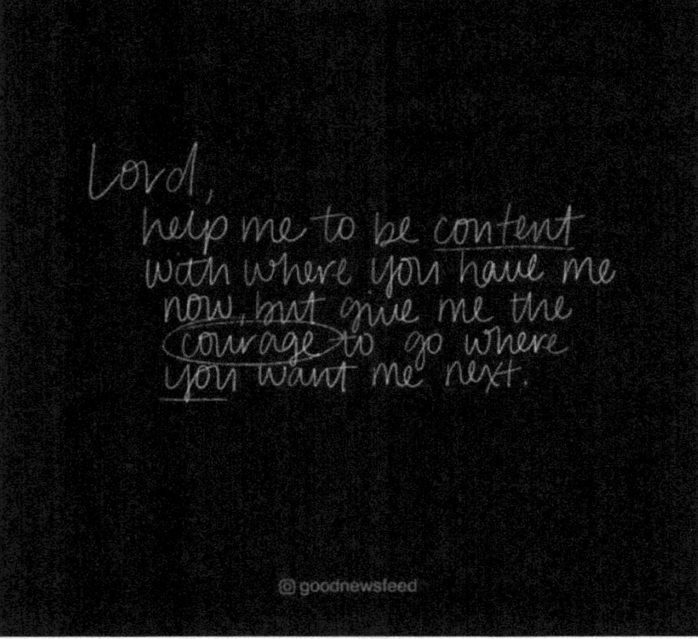

Crystal Gowen
July 20, 2019 ·

Between my puffy eye, sciatica, lack of sleep, and we l the whole recovery process....I need God tonight.

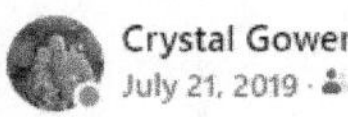

Crystal Gowen
July 21, 2019 ·

Prayers please. Went to Duke Raleigh as the right side of my face has become swollen. They believe it to be an angioedema. Cause is unknown. Will be following up with Dr. Friedman tomorrow. My spirit y'all...the Devil is trying it. Brain Tumor Warrior- Crystal's Journey

Crystal Gowen
July 24, 2019 ·
Brain Tumor Warrior- Crystal's Journey

Once you walk through pain, you may never be able to unsee pain again. It's all over us, and on her face, and in his voice. At first, this will feel like a chink in your armor. But later, this will become your armor. And you will walk straight into the thick of someone else's pain because Jesus Christ walked into yours.

@THEPAIGEPIPPIN

Crystal Gowen
July 24, 2019 ·

Hello FB it's Cameron here again . I just want everyone to keep Crystal in your thoughts and prayers as she going into surgery at Duke as we speak . Just a minor setback from here previous surgery last month. She was having some swelling in her head due to an infection so Dr is going back in to clean area and make sure there is nothing else going on . Thanks for all the good vibe y'all can send our way!! Brain Tumor Warrior- Crystal's Journey

Lord,

Help me I'm Worn. This journey has me worn. So much has happened in such a short period of time. Thank you for the blessings you have given me. My soul needs relief. It yearns for peace and my body seeks your healing. This is more than a physical journey as I need prayers for the spirit.

Amen.

I'm Tired I'm worn
My heart is heavy
From the work it takes
To keep on breathing
I've made mistakes
I've let my hope fail
My soul feels crushed
By the weight of this world
And I know that you can give me rest
So I cry out with all that I have left
Let me see redemption win
Let me know the struggle ends
That you can mend a heart
That's frail and torn

I wanna know a song can rise
From the ashes of a broken life
And all that's dead inside can be reborn
Cause I'm worn
I know I need to lift my eyes up
But I'm too weak
Life just won't let up
And I know that you can give me rest
So I cry out with all that I have left
Let me see redemption win
Let me know the struggle ends
That you can mend a heart
That's frail and torn

I wanna know a song can rise
From the ashes of a broken life
And all that's dead inside can be reborn
Cause I'm worn
My prayers are wearing thin
Yeah, I'm worn
Even before the day begins
Yeah, I'm worn
I've lost my will to fight
I'm worn
So, heaven come and flood my eyes

Crystal Gowen
August 6, 2019 ·

As my recovery continues, my testimony grows. The road I tarry has been long and difficult. There are still good and bad days, both physically and mentally. Yet, I rise. As I read the book of Psalms, I cry out to God. He hears me and daily, I see a blessing....no matter big or small. Continue to pray for me. Specifically, my PICC line stays clear from infection, the medicine heals the infection, my incision remains clear of infection, and for my spirit. I am grateful for the prayers, love, and support. Brain Tumor Warrior- Crystal's Journey

So give me faith like Daniel in the lion's den
Give me hope like Moses in the wilderness
Give me a heart like David, Lord be my defense
So I can face my giants with confidence
I'm gonna sing and shout and shake the walls
I won't stop until I see 'em fall
Gonna stand up, step out when you call
Jesus, Jesus

"Confidence" Sanctus Real

This spoke to me today.
Brain Tumor Warrior- Crystal's Journey

Testimony: The Lord has seen my broken spirit and never wants His child to be in sorrow. Yet, he sends messages like on the wings of a dove. Today, I received a special card in the mail full of scriptures, a phone call from a friend, and my daily visit from Mama. In all these situations, I testify that God will bring me through this and my spirit will be healed. He will send blessings to help guide me. Brain Tumor Warrior- Crystal's Journey

Update: Stitches are out. Everything is healing nicely. Prayers needed to keep infection away, PICC line stays infection free, medication continues to work, and for my spirit. The emotional toll this recovery process will be my testimony one day, but the devil stays busy and I need to make sure he's rebuked! For those I reached out to last night (yesterday was an incredibly hard day), thank you for praying for me and for the words of encouragement. I know God has this! Brain Tumor Warrior- Crystal's Journey

Cause I'm just a nobody
Trying to tell everybody
All about Somebody who saved my soul
Ever since You rescued me
You gave my heart a song to sing
I'm living for the world to see
Nobody but Jesus
I'm living for the world to see
Nobody but Jesus
Brain Tumor Warrior- Crystal's Journey

Update: I'm back at Duke. They're running lots of test, but I need prayers for the blood cultures to remain free of growth, white blood count to keep going up, and all blood work related to go up. Mama is here with me as Cameron is with the kids this time. They need him and he's handling school stuff. They're my rocks! No growth in the cultures means no more IV line and a pill regiment. We are speaking this in existence. I ask you to do the same. Thanks for all of your support. Brain Tumor Warrior- Crystal's Journey

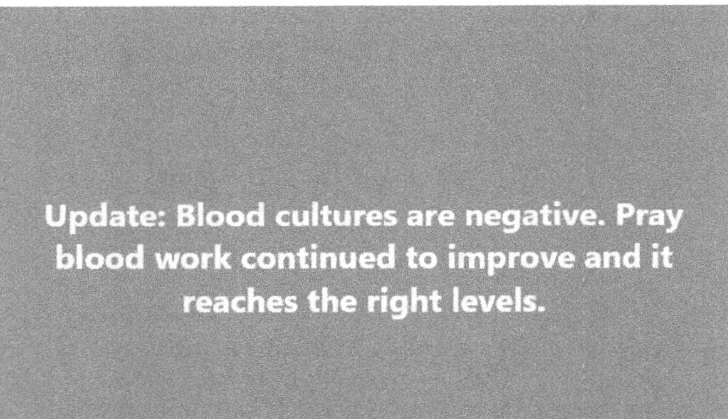

Thank you all the prayers. I am being discharged. Please continue to pray in the coming days for added strength, recovery, and peace. Brain Tumor Warrior- Crystal's Journey

Crystal Gowen
August 29, 2019 ·

I declare God will see this blood work drawn today will improve! My results are covered. Brain Tumor Warrior- Crystal's Journey

Crystal Gowen
August 30, 2019 ·

The doctor has prescribed a weekend of fun. My counts are back up. Iron deficient, but it's a lot better than where I was last week. Prayers are working! I've been told to claim it in His name....even though I'm struggling...I'm claiming recovery. Brain Tumor Warrior- Crystal's Journey

Crystal Gowen
September 2, 2019 ·

Gotta claim blood draw #2 is just as good as last week and my appointment at Duke goes well Friday.

GOD SAID:

I need you to get excited again. I need you to remember you're not in this thing alone. I'm working on your challenges, I've already assigned angels to you. So let go of the stress & just trust Me; I've got a pretty incredible ending in store. In fact, that's why you need to get excited again... because the happy ending I've got coming, is going to **ROCK. YOUR. WORLD.**

Crystal Gowen
September 3, 2019 ·

Praise the Lord my labs today came back good!!!

HEAL ME, O LORD,
AND I SHALL BE HEALED;
SAVE ME, AND I SHALL
BE SAVED.

JEREMIAH 17:14

Crystal Gowen
September 12, 2019

I'm asking for prayers again. My appointment with Infectious Disease (a follow-up from the infection in July they surgically removed and I was on antibiotics for and from my neutropenic episode). My last labs were normal and the blood cultures taken in the hospital were negative...meaning no sign of infection. Please join me in prayer over this appointment as we want them to turn me loose.

this is what the
LORD
says:
I have heard
your prayer
AND I will
heal you

20:5

Crystal Gowen
September 13, 2019

Testify!! My chapter with Infectious Disease clinic is over! The doctor's note stated I am infection free. I know God will see to it that it will not return.

Crystal Gowen
September 16, 2019

I'm claiming my MRI results will be good!!! Friday is the MRI and next Tuesday is post op! Hear me O God!!! I want to be able to testify! Amen!

Crystal Gowen
September 20, 2019

MRI complete...
Now we wait...
Tuesday can't get here soon enough!
Praising my God for bringing me this far!

Crystal Gowen
September 22, 2019

For the first time in my life, I've prayed like never before. I'm praying for the MRI results to be good. God saved me from a brain tumor. God saved me from an infection. Got saved me from neutropenia. God has saved me by grace. I know this is just the beginning of lifelong MRIs, but God is good. Shouting to the Lord, he will make sure there's nothing left of my tumor, there's no infection lingering, there's no more complications, anxiety and depression will flee from me, and that it'll never come back. Jesus, I'm giving you my burdens because the road is long and I'm weary. To my prayer warriors, I thank God for you every day because when I was at my lowest...you lifted me up.

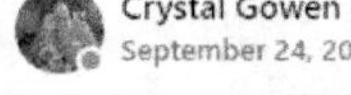

Crystal Gowen is with **Brandie Black** and **Lois Edwards**.
September 24, 2019

Praise Report: My MRI results showed the tumor was completely removed, nothing left behind. My doctor said, "I'm healed" and I can get back to normal. I'm cured from Ted the tumor, the infection, and neutropenia. He will see me in a year to continually monitor me, which is standard after brain tumors. My God is GOOD!!! I've struggled in many ways, but I'm thankful God sent me prayer warriors to keep me uplifted when I was low. This is the hardest journey I've made in life and I was complimented by my doctor as he called me a "strong woman". I'll have a battle scar and dent in my forehead (the latter he offered to repair later, but I'll be keeping it). Praying I'll not have a reoccurrence (it's a low percentage). Thank you God!!!! I praise your Holy Name! God saved my life in more ways than one!
Brain Tumor Warrior- Crystal's Journey

Crystal Gowen
September 24, 2019 ·

This man has endured a lot through this journey. It was never a journey he left me alone to travel, and one that at times he helped carry me through because the road was too long and I was weary. He has wiped my tears, tried to help calm my worries, and took on the roles I couldn't fulfill at times. He has been the rock I needed, my safe place, and my smile or laughter when the days were bleak. He amazes me every day and he never once complained about this journey...our journey. When I thought I couldn't love you more, you never left my side. When the days turned into months, you were there to inject medication, make meals, tend to the kids, and put in a full day's work. God has blessed me with far more than I could ever imagine. I'm so thankful tonight. Grace saved me. Hope anchored me. Love surrounded me. Faith, even as tiny as a mustard seed, sustained me. All these given to us by God on this journey. Keeping us strong to carry on. How blessed I am!!! How blessed we all are to serve a wonderful God. Amen.

Brain Tumor Warrior- Crystal's Journey

Crystal Gowen is with **Brandie Black**.
September 24, 2019 ·

I'm thankful you were on this journey with me. From chicken salad, phone calls, Snapchats, and knowing if I needed you just to talk...you'd be there. There's no one who could get away with breathing in my face as I'm trying to wake up from surgery just to see if I could still smell, who could sit by my bedside knowing it was not the way I intended on spending my birthday, and who would tell me not to give up because I was strong enough to make it through all this. God knew I needed you all along.

♥ Big Sis

Brain Tumor Warrior- Crystal's Journey

Crystal Gowen is with **Nickolas Gowen** and **2 others**.
September 24, 2019 ·

These wonderful amazing kiddos....they have done so much to keep me encouraged, motivated, and surrounded in love throughout this journey. They've matured this summer in ways that I'm so proud, stepping up and helping out, working together, and selflessly sacrificing increments of being kids to make sure I was ok. They're the most amazing kids and I love them more than words could say. God blessed me to play a role in their lives as a Mama or Bonus Mama and I couldn't be more grateful. Brain Tumor Warrior- Crystal's Journey

+5

Mama,

You're the call I can make in the dark of night knowing you'll be right over. You catch the tears that have stricken my face etched in lines of worry. You have stroked my hair, combed it, and washed it as if I were a youngster still in your care. No, age doesn't matter. Whether I was four or forty, it hasn't mattered. You have prayed over me, for me, and requested them on my behalf. You summoned up prayer warriors in our family, church, and community. You never lost sight of God and carried pockets full of mustard seeds....planting firmly in fields of faith. Just a little talk with Jesus and you were firmly standing on the faith of His Word. In my darkness, you were my light. The light of God shown through diminishing what the Devil wanted to keep hidden...hope, love, and faith. You preached in person, on the phone, and in Facebook posts you were sure would make me stop to ponder. You were here always. You took care of our babies and finally during my last stay...you took care of me 1:1. When I thought in life the roles would be reversed...there you were sleeping in a chair alongside my bed, making sure I ate, helping me bathe my weary body, and wiping my tears away. You never gave up and were determined to make sure I didn't either. Whenever I needed you...you were there. Planting mustard seeds of faith all around me. Never letting me pull them out of the ground, but guiding me to watch, wait, and see how God would make them grow. I'll never be too old to need you. I love you.

Brain Tumor Warrior- Crystal's Journey

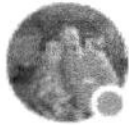

Crystal Gowen is with **Danny Garris** and **Gail Garris**.
September 25, 2019 ·

Leaving for surgery that morning, I clenched my Daddy's hand and cried...not for me....but for him. Knowing he was worried. No one wants to see their children, even if they're grown, go through this journey. In that moment, I told my Daddy I loved him. I loved him for being my Daddy, for giving me unconditional love through all my decisions in life (even the lousy ones), for giving me his last name, and always being there for me. God has blessed me in more ways than I can count. He gave my Daddy a chance to love again and have a love with Gail. She's been my Daddy's rock through this journey, too. We couldn't have done it without her. From goodies, phone calls, visits, and keeping us all motivated. God has blessed us! Amen!

Brain Tumor Warrior- Crystal's Journey

Crystal Gowen
September 27, 2019 ·

Day 3: Joy. Not an emotion. It's God right in front of you. Grace. Hope. Love. Faith. It's being able to accept the journey. Sort it all out. Laugh at the sprigs of hair you're blessed to have no matter how out of control they are. Maybe they're a sign of mustard seeds sprouting up from the ground after the storm. Smile. Knowing prayer works. Knowing it comes from a place of Christ's love. Yes, joy....that's what I am striving for. Brain Tumor Warrior- Crystal's Journey

Crystal Gowen
September 27, 2019 ·

Low iron....
Recheck in 4-6 weeks
Praying for improvement...
Hope these supplements work or it's a transfusion. My God's got this!!!

The hardest realization in this journey is just how dark some days were. The best realization is just how far God carried me and never stopped loving me. Nothing prepares you for a journey like this, but I'm sure praising God for the preparations he made. He saved me. The sun shines brighter, the rain falls lighter, and even the clouds can't sway my day. I prayed for peace many times and the peace I have isn't half of what I imagined. It's more. Brain Tumor Warrior- Crystal's Journey

Crystal Gowen is with **Nickolas Gowen** and **5 others**.
November 12, 2019 ·

From the first pic...I didn't even know Ted the Tumor existed. The next day would change my life. I couldn't phathom a brain tumor had been lurking the past six years! I had planned my funeral knowing this could be the end of my story. Humor was the best way to find my way through the first surgery, but humor only goes so far. My darkest days set in recovering from surgery number two. What had I done wrong?! How did I get this infection?! Why was God allowing this to happen?!? Would I ever be healed or would it keep dragging out?! I cried out "Lord! Don't forsake me! I am here Lord. I need you! What do you want me to do?" I cried for weeks. My joy dismantled and the Devil set in with depressive, lost thoughts. I read the Word. My pastor suggested Psalms. I read. I cried. I pleaded. I read more. I turned page after page and felt the weight of my darkness. My PICC line medication caused my immune system to dwindle into tenths of percentage. I returned to the hospital for the last time. I had spent weeks obsessing how to prevent infection. I was afraid to be around anyone. I couldn't hug my kids or my husband. I was stripped of the things that were the very essence of me. Even when I got good news, the Devil whispered in my ear. The darkness engulfed me. I was anxious. God's fight to keep my soul was real. I could feel the battle and the more He fought for it, the more the Devil tormented me. He sought one over the ninety-nine. He wasn't going to lose me. Doctor appointments seemed unbearable, even though they yielded good news. At the end of September, I was informed the tumor had been completely resected, nothing left behind. No infection. I was healed the doctor said. What I had prayed for had been revealed. I have to return yearly for scans, but prayer is part of my daily life. The Word is part of my daily life. I witness using my story. I hope it brings someone closer to God. Through my darkness, he carried me. He sent prayer warriors to pray for me. Mama was here to rebuke the Devil, by God's divine intervention I'm sure. Cameron, by my side, carrying out his vows. My children praying and helping out. So many people God put in my life. I'm here today because of God. He wasn't done with my story. Today, I can smile because I have joy. Not happiness, but joy. I know my arms should be stretched out where Jesus' were, but He died for my sins, so that I can live to tell my story.

Brain Tumor Warrior- Crystal's Journey

Crystal Gowen
November 25, 2019 ·

Awaiting God's answer. Prayers it's His will. Faithful no matter the answer.

Crystal Gowen
November 27, 2019 ·

The hardest part of my journey is being comfortable with my outside appearance. My hair is growing back, but I know there's a hefty scar underneath. It's growing back a different shade with more wisdom tones than the rest of it. It grows in a different manner than it did before and at best I try to style it. It takes a lot of courage to wear it proudly. There was a time it was riddled with staples and stitches, cut into twice, washed with baby shampoo, and always air dried. It's come a long way, but I'm still a woman, even with the courage I display, knows what I see in the mirror. It's not what it used to be. I have faith it will be one day and that's where my courage derives. I stepped out in courage to take family pictures in our Christmas jammies to signify that while I see the reflection in the mirror as is ... the faith within shines through. I can't thank you enough Lauren Tant for making me feel courageous enough to take pictures no matter the current #braintumorhair I have. They're beautiful and I can't wait to see the rest.
Brain Tumor Warrior- Crystal's Journey

Crystal Gowen
November 28, 2019 ·

Happy 18th birthday Nickolas Gowen !! I'm so proud of you and all you have accomplished. You're a role model to your siblings and you're fiercely protective of them all. I'm so blessed to be in your life. Having you as a bonus son makes my heart complete. I'm so grateful for the memories we've made. I couldn't imagine sharing my bucket list of seeing Paul McCartney with anyone else. Your decision to serve our country makes me beam with pride. It just shows the incredible young man you are and continue to be. You remind me so much of your Dad as you care deeply for others, especially Kristin Currie. Your relationship goals remind me of the old soul that you carry within. Continue to let God's light shine through. I hope your day is amazing! I love you!

Crystal Gowen
November 28, 2019 ·

I'm grateful to share Thanksgiving with my family, friends, and fur babies! No matter what, be grateful, be blessed, and love always!

I haven't posted my daily thanks because I wanted to share my reflections:
I rise every morning thankful for another day to share with my husband, children, family, and friends. I'm grateful God blessed me to survive a brain tumor to share each day with those I share my life. My purpose is to share positivity whenever I can and reduce moments of the flesh. My goal is to help another in need and not only share wisdom, but take it in. I walk into my workplace with a newfound purpose to share self-care, so we can be the best at what we do and support our team in their daily tasks. I pray with conviction for those I love and cherish. I let the ache flow for those I miss and have gone before me, instead of keeping it behind a wall. I strive for co-parenting goals, even when we differ. I'm blessed to share my children with my husband and share in the lives of his. I'm blessed to be in the lives of Riley's older brothers despite our geographically distance. Blood doesn't define our family. It's never defined my own. My heart is grateful, enduring, and forever faithful! That's what I'm thankful for this year.

Crystal Gowen
December 6, 2019 ·

Days..What are these? The overwhelming struggle to want to be the girl you have pictured in your head...the one that smiled, was ready for an adventure, and was oblivious to any feelings like she has now. How hard it feels to keep up with how fast life moves and all you want is for the weekend to be here...to enjoy it with those you love and were divided from at one point...the ache it caused and how you desperately want to make up for lost time...how hard it is to get the words out and recognizing there's a numb feeling there where feelings should be...how you want it to be the picture in your head and not feel less than who you used to be....when loud noises, bright lights, fast paces, etc. didn't bother you before...when you felt pretty, smart, and fun. In some instances feeling robbed of your identity. Yeah those days come and go...making you feel like you were over the hill just to see another mountain to climb. Lord, give me strength. I stand faithful.
Brain Tumor Warrior- Crystal's Journey

Crystal Gowen
December 16, 2019 ·

God's spirit fell over me...
I lived to see another day...
Another birthday to celebrate with Miss Ashleigh.
Thank you God!
If you don't know Jesus as your Savior....know that a baby was born to die for our sins and did so selflessly. There's no sin he cannot wash unclean...no heart he can't mend...and no person He can't love. John 3:16

Crystal Gowen
December 17, 2019 ·

Chronicles of Surviving a Brain Tumor:

Y'all the Devil has been hard at work on me. As crazy as this sounds, I started experiencing cold like symptoms. This is my first ordeal since the brain surgery where I have a common illness. Now you may ask how the devil is busy with something simple as a cold? Wellllllll....I wish it was that easy. It triggered my anxiety and I was hit with an emotional breakdown today. It hit me out of nowhere and my mood changed. It progressed from there as I saw my Mom's former WilMed Nursing Home co-workers eating out for their Christmas lunch and thought she should be there. Mind you I was doing the same. My cold symptoms are pretty tame like I don't feel bad per se...postnasal stuff, stuffy/runny nose at times, etc. It's like day 5 and I went from having a cough and sore throat to some gross mucous in the a.m. to clear throughout the day without meds. The devil is busy because I'm anxious about being sick with a cold....like what if it's more?!? The fact that I had this episode coupled with missing Mom...it ended in a tearful, snotty mess. I'm better now. I reached my hand up to God and asked him for his peace, for his healing, and cried out.... Then I called Mama...where I found peace in knowing that there are days like these, that the devil is busy, and I have to stop, pray, and take a breath and know that God has it. As for missing my Mom, well Mama said time doesn't take away the ache and you'll miss things. If you could say a little prayer for me, I'd appreciate it. Brain Tumor Warrior- Crystal's Journey

Crystal Gowen
December 31, 2019 ·

Y'all know I believe in prayer...
I have a follow-up appointment with my regular MD on 1/2/20. Praying for my iron levels to be where they need to be and all other tests to be good. Brain Tumor Warrior- Crystal's Journey

Crystal Gowen
January 1, 2020 ·

2019: It was a year of lessons, survival, faith, and ultimately love. At the beginning of the year, God had us work on our marriage to prepare us for what lay ahead. We grew stronger and committed time for us. We cherished making memories with our children, family, and friends. Riley Tulppo turned thirteen in April and we celebrated. We spent spring break with Uncle Tommy and Aunt Pam. By mid-year, Nickolas Gowen and I saw Paul McCartney in concert; crossing off one of our bucket lists. The next day I was diagnosed with a meningioma brain tumor who I named Ted. Surgery occured in June. Friends and family shared their love and support and brought food made with love. Our church family supported us. Our Pastor K. Darrel Bowles stayed with Cameron as I underwent my surgery. My Daddy, Gail Garris, Brandie Black, Uncle JB, Mama, Pamela Ballance Edwards were there keeping us in prayer. Countless cards arrived and blessed us with their prayers and thoughts. My family rallied from near and far to pray. Congregations in various churches prayed. Cameron Gowen devoted himself just as he vowed to do when we married. God worked on my faith. I battled the worst depression I ever faced. My Mama, Lois Edwards, helped take care of me just as she did when I was a child. Carolyn Davis Bunn kept us uplifted and encouraged. Our children pitched in, matured quickly, and gave it their all. Gracie turned eleven in the midst of my diagnosis. Nickolas was sworn into the USAF and will leave in August 2020. I turned forty on the OR table as the team at Duke removed an infection from my surgical incision in July. God blessed us with a wonderful team of doctors at Duke who I'm incredibly grateful. Ted was removed completely and was benign. In August, I was re-hospitalized due to neutropenia from the antibiotic in my PICC line. September brought us joyous news as I return yearly for MRI scans. We worked on improving my iron levels, self care, and returning to the team I love at Eastpointe. Senior events and pictures occured for both Nickolas and Ashleigh. My faith restored and our focus is on God's blessings. We celebrated Nickolas turning eighteen and Ashleigh turning seventeen in November and December, respectively. We rescued a dog, Candy, who is my side kick. Kristin Kristin Gowen taught us to make homemade Butterfingers. Nickolas shared in a small birthday celebration with friends. Ashleigh shared her birthday with family. We enjoyed Thanksgiving and Christmas. My sister and Bobby hosted their first annual Friendsgiving and Christmas and we enjoyed the fellowship. Gracie and Ashleigh Carico helped make cookies for the members of our church. We attended our church's Christmas program and Christmas Eve service. Christmas morning we hosted brunch and shared it with Mama, Ma, Pa Bunn, Tim, Daddy, Gail, Mike Garris, Kelly Garris, Kaelin, and Carter. We revelled in time with family and friends. We prayed, testified, and shared our love. Our year ended with a date and celebrating the new year with Tim. We survived because of God. We stand firmly on His promises. Satan did not win. We are still writing our story. Here's to 2020! Chronicles of a Brain Tumor Warrior-Crystal's Journey

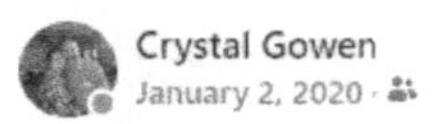

Crystal Gowen
January 2, 2020 ·

I need a WORD
January 2, 2020 ·

PRAYER FOR HEALTH

Father,

I come to you today in total thanksgiving and gratitude for how far you've brought me. There are many persons that were born on the same day with me but are no more. In your infinite love and wisdom, you have preserved me not because I deserve it but because of your unconditional love. Even if my whole body is full of mouths, it still won't be enough to praise you. You have done me so well and am truly grateful. Into your hands Lord, I commit my health because your word says that whatever we commit to your hands is taken care of. I ask for a perfect health. I declare that every part of my body works perfectly. I curse every root of sickness in my life and I proclaim that I am healed and made whole from every infirmity. My body is the temple of God; therefore, sickness is not permitted to dwell in this body. Your word says that if I serve you, you'll bless my bread and my water and take away sickness from my midst. I believe you Lord and I know that affliction shall never arise a second time. I declare today that everyone connected to me enjoys good health and vitality. We shall not cast our young and there shall be no loss. So shall it be in Jesus name, amen.

Crystal Gowen is with Lois Edwards.
January 2, 2020 ·

My doctor has now classified me officially as "post meningioma resection". While she said it cannot be guaranteed, it is likely the tumor will not reoccur given the pathology report. She spent 30 minutes talking to me about...well me. It was by far the most positive encounter to date (aside from Dr. Friedman saying it was gone and nothing was leftover).

The lab closed before my appointment ended, but I'll be there bright and early to have them drawn. God has provided thus far and I believe he will do it again! No matter the outcome, He has a plan.

Mama, thank you for going with me. No matter how old I get, having you there means the world to me. Chronicles of a Brain Tumor Warrior- Crystal's Journey

Where
God guides,
He provides

ISAIAH 58:11

Crystal Gowen
January 6, 2020

When I tell you my God is good, He has heard my prayers!
Labs are back. Levels are up! Now waiting to hear from the MD for continuity of care!!

Crystal Gowen
January 9, 2020

It's growing y'all!!!
#90sbangs
#braintumorhair
Chronicles of a Brain Tumor Warrior- Crystal's Journey

Crystal Gowen
January 11, 2020 ·

These bangs tho....
#curlyhair
#lookwhatmybraintumorleftme
#braintumorhair
#snapchatfun
Chronicles of a Brain Tumor Warrior- Crystal's Journey

Crystal Gowen
January 11, 2020 ·

Old Salem with my BFFs...
I started out with straight hair, but we met some rain...
And my hair isn't two-tone, but these pics tho....lol
Spending time with my girls is good for the soul.

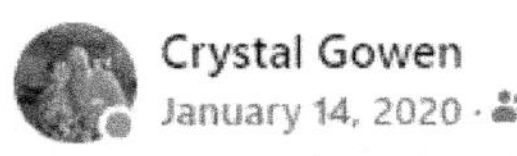

Crystal Gowen
January 14, 2020

I gazed upon the depths
Murky and shallow
Lapping across wounds
Piercing with ache as the salt situated upon the grooves of my scar
Long and etched
Raised and curved
By and by
The slow agony of being torn

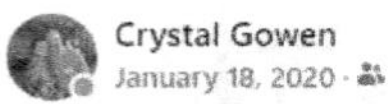

Crystal Gowen
January 18, 2020

The echo of young love enveloped the chambers of my soul...
To and fro...
Like winds of change...
We caress the lines of founding love...
Tarrying along this embarked road...
Never alone...
Side by side...
Forever more...
The tides of my soul roar like an echo from long ago...
Firmly planted and etched into my memory...
Drawn like water, crisp, and fulfilling...
How our love has grown.
Faces of children so long ago, yet a reflection that never ceases to exist...
Love never dies...
It yields growth every year, along the lines of life's mark.
Truest love is like a flood from the depths we will never part. ♥

Crystal Gowen
January 22, 2020

This....
Those beautiful nurses at Duke in July 2019, played Christian music using the cell phone. We three sang as they prepped me for my second surgery. #whenGodmakesafootprint Chronicles of a Brain Tumor Warrior- Crystal's Journey

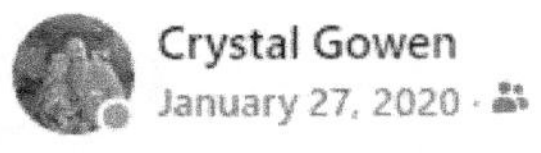

Chronicles of a Brain Tumor Survivor:

We are headed to Shriner's Hospital in Greenville, SC today. Being a Mama never stops. No matter what happens, I'm her biggest supporter and strongest advocate. Her annual appointment to check the status of her legs. Those beautiful legs they repaired almost ten years ago. I'm thankful for the Shriner's Roadrunners (Mr. Tony and Mr. JB) for our trip today.

Post brain tumor, I thank God I can make this trip with her. This journey began twelve years ago and God has blessed her so! I know God is always writing my story and He isn't done with me yet. There's a young lady who needs her Mama. Chronicles of a Brain Tumor Warrior- Crystal's Journey

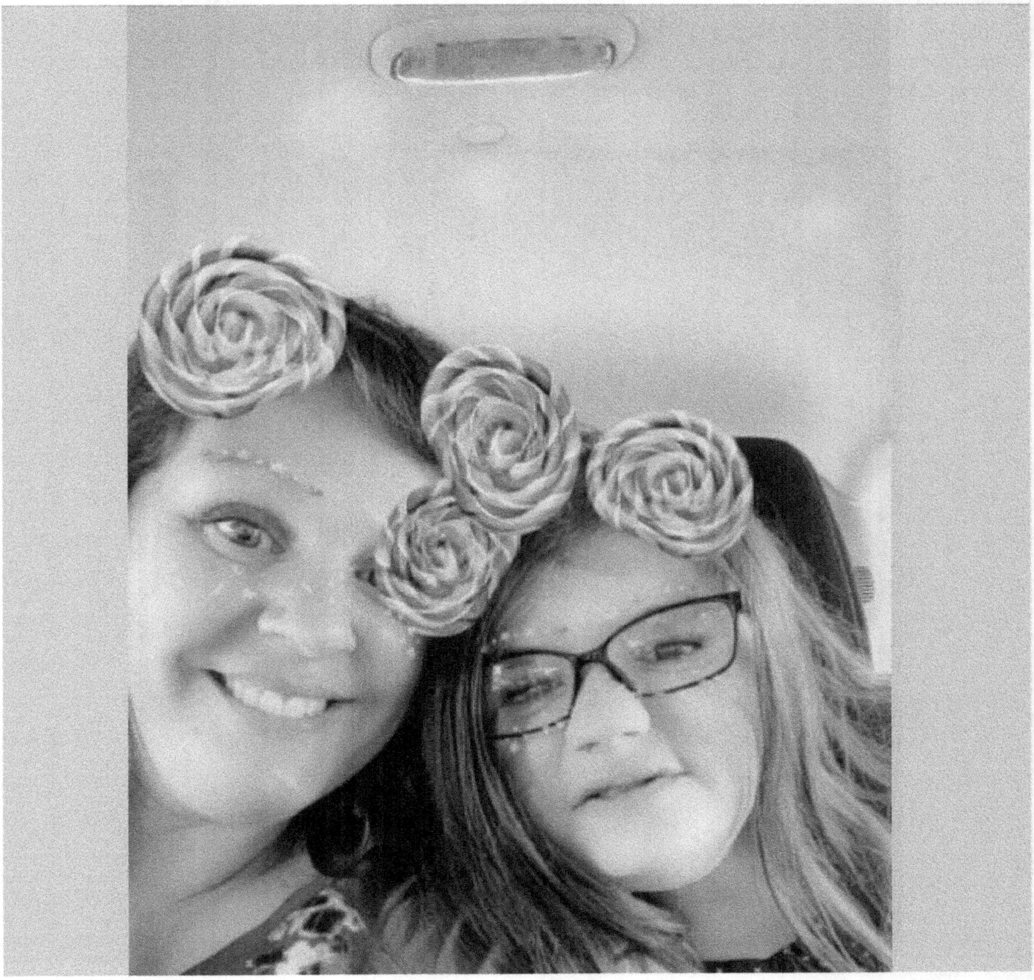

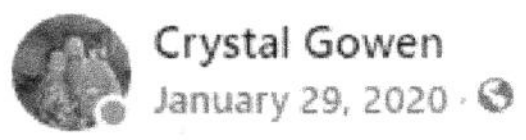

Crystal Gowen
January 29, 2020 ·

Chronicles of a Brain Tumor Survivor....

I felt this deep in my core. The friends that bring you movies and M&M's and laugh along with your antics of how surgery has left you looking like you got a face lift out of the deal, share hair bands and tips to help you style the freshly shaven already been cut one time scar, call you when the PICC line didn't work and wiped your immune system out because they can't see you in person, and take day trips to share in your love for history all the while complimenting you on your Winona Ryder bangs. They're protective of how you ascend and descend stairs and navigate uneven pavement. They don't treat you like lost something, even though you know things are different. They love the new version just as much as the old. In fact, most days text messages and calls are the best therapy of all. They're a reflection of who you were and who you are still loving you all the while in the bond you've shared. They encourage you to let what's missing shine....to let your scar tell the story...and share what makes them love you so much. Chronicles of a Brain Tumor Warrior- Crystal's Journey

What is Love?
By Emma K. Age 6

Love is when you're
missing some of your
teeth
but you're not afraid to
smile
because you know your
friends will still love you
even though some of you
is missing

♡

Crystal Gowen is with **Lois Edwards**.
February 4, 2020 ·

Chronicles of a Brain Tumor Survivor...

"And I wished grandpas never died"

For 24 years, I have wished this exact sentiment. Each year it feels just as raw as the day it happened. This year it feels raw, yet different. My relationship with God has changed and more than ever I believe I'll see him in Heaven and days like today...I can't wait. Brad Paisley wrote a song with the lyric "When I get to Heaven I'll walk with my grandaddy"...well that is exactly what I want to do. You see the ache of missing him is still there...strong as ever...and going through life without him these past 24 years doesn't make it go away...it leaves a void. Papa was a legend in my eyes and at 40...faults and all...he always will be. I was Papa's girl....his Puddinghead...and let's face it... I was his sidekick and proud of it. Lol. Watching him fall sick to strokes and other problems was tough. I wasn't even a teen when he went to the hospital a few days and wouldn't come home. He went to a nursing home and it crushed me. I was angry at the world because I wanted him home. I remember begging my Mom and saying I'd help take care of him, but the reality was he was too sick to come home. So, I went to the nursing home. I spent time there to help Mama, so she could work or even get away...because she spent her time between there and the shop. I shared lunches, watched westerns, and helped him with anything he asked. Mama always left some money in his PJ pocket and looking back I reckon he probably had a little something to do with that...he would give me the money to get a soda or some snack out of the machine. Lots of times we split a candy bar or nabs. I relish in those memories because they were between he and I. He made it to 70 that January... something he aspired to do. I remember a week before taking my SATs, I went to the hospital to relieve Mama, so she could go back to work. Of course, he wanted to know how school was going and then he talked to me about dying. He asked me could he...like I had a say...and it's probably the most unselfish thing I ever did in this life....I said yes....even though I wanted to say no, you can't....but I knew he had suffered so much. His body had been in pain. He had endured and he was tired. All these years later and having that pivotal dream while surgery...I realize he was just trying to cushion the blow of missing him. He didn't want to leave any more than I wanted him to go. Yet, he knew it was time. He will always have a big chunk of my heart. He will always be in the place that protects the innocence only letting it surface every once in a while. He's in the memories of a girl who became a woman that survived a brain tumor. He was in a dream that said...You can't stay here. Your work isn't done. He's in everything I do and frankly he's the foundation of why I do what I do.

He shares Heaven with my Mom and while I hope that day is a long time coming...To see them together with our Heavenly Father is just where I want to be.

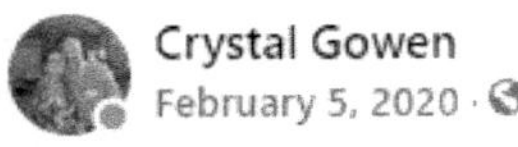
Crystal Gowen
February 5, 2020 ·

Chronicles of a Brain Tumor Survivor...

Sometimes you just need a sister session at lunch with your baby sister. You just need to bounce how you feel off of each other. You need to drink cider and eat a mini muffin in a place most people don't even know is SO good. Somehow it makes the day better. You have a perspective and at the same time you share a common bond. You can talk about how you feel and be totally honest. You listen, so the other person can be heard. At the end, you can shake it off even for only an hour. It also signals the move into adulthood as the topics are more mature. Yep, send a text- Wanna go to lunch?
Chronicles of a Brain Tumor Warrior- Crystal's Journey

Sometimes the results can be the best therapy ever. Love you Brandie Black

Crystal Gowen
February 10, 2020 ·

Chronicles of a Brain Tumor Survivor...

Pray...
God is faithful...
Even when it's our darkest hour...

I wished brain tumors, or any tumor for that matter never existed. It's a hard journey. When I learn one more person has been affected or has undergone this journey... tumors, cancer, etc. My heart breaks. I know the journey is hard. Some days it feels like the worst Hell you could ever imagine. Not just for yourself, but for the loved ones going alongside you. It's a fight worth fighting...against every odd counted against you.

I remember every prayer I prayed and those I heard over me. I remember praying for my dear friend JoAnn A. Langley who underwent surgery within weeks of mine. Prayer is still a continuous road I travel. If you have a need for prayer, raise your hand in the comment. I'll pray for you! PM me. I'll pray for you! I'll pray for those who may not be able to acknowledge prayer, but today I will pray for you!

God be with us all.
Chronicles of a Brain Tumor Warrior- Crystal's Journey

Crystal Gowen
February 16, 2020 ·

Chronicles of a Brain Tumor Survivor....

Old Man Winter has chilled the days of late causing my scar to be tender. Simply, everything is contracting and the awoken nerves don't care for the feeling. I'm out sporting my beanies. Hair is tied up to make life simpler. Tonight, as I wait for my grocery order (I am finding that grocery pickup allows me to grab minutes I typically wouldn't have had), to spend time with my Gracie Lou Who. She makes my heart smile and keeps me inspired. She's picked out a frame this evening to put her sister photo in. Lord, I'm thankful for this day, even the tenderness that reminds me of a difficult time.
Chronicles of a Brain Tumor Warrior- Crystal's Journey

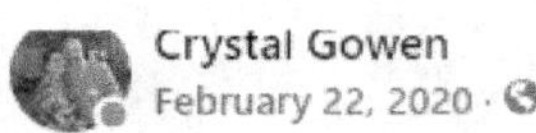

Crystal Gowen
February 22, 2020 ·

Chronicles of a Brain Tumor Survivor...

I saw a friend last night that I hadn't seen in a while. It was wonderful seeing her and she spoke words that resonated with my heart. It's powerful when others join in prayer for you, your situation, and your family. How wonderful His grace is. How pure is His love. No matter where I'm out or how long it's been---8 months since resection-- I see God's love in the words of others. More so, she reminded me I was a survivor. I don't recognize myself as one most days, but today...I woke up and remembered it was a battle that God fought. My pages are still turning and knowing I've got friends, whether we talk often or not, like that shows God at work standing on his promises.

Thanks Tiffany Glover! Your words of encouragement were uplifting! It was wonderful to see you last night.
Chronicles of a Brain Tumor Warrior- Crystal's Journey

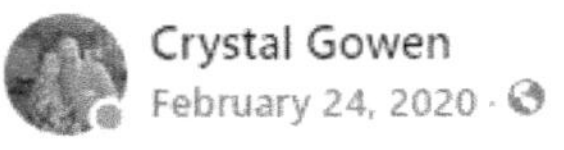

Crystal Gowen
February 24, 2020 ·

I did a thing yesterday...
Something familiar from that old life...
That connection that draws Cameron and I close...
Gently gliding through the curves and straightaways...
As the scenery passes us by peacefully...
Cameron's arm draped over my knee, leaned back...
All my cares fleeting...
Just he and I...
Our place...
Where we meet to intertwine.

#fourwheelsmovesthebodytwowheelsmovesthesoul
Chronicles of a Brain Tumor Warrior- Crystal's Journey

Crystal Gowen
February 27, 2020 ·

This....
How many times I remember crying out...
Grief and sorrow in hand....
Thank God for blessing me to share my story.

The Unraveling by Kelli Bachara
February 25, 2020 ·

Psalm 88 is straight up SAD.

It talks about crying out to the Lord all day and night. It explains a "soul full of trouble" and being in the "lowest pit" and "darkest depths."
In fact, it ends with "the darkness is my closest friend."

These words sound like they came from a broken heart. It sounds like someone who was experiencing grief and perhaps trauma.

It sounds like someone who felt like God had abandoned them.

They couldn't even finish off the Psalm on a hopeful note. It ended with mourning and darkness.

And sometimes that's how it goes. We can't wrap up our current situation in a pretty bow. We can't find the bright side.

All we can do is go to God and honestly pour out our aching hearts.

Sometimes.

There does come a time though, when we feel our chin being lifted upward as the Lord wants us to meet His gaze.

He doesn't tell us to put our brokenness away. He doesn't tell us to get over it.

He tells us to come. Just as we are. Grief, trauma, fear.. all of it.

He reminds us who He is. He reminds us what He has already done.

It's no surprise that the very next Psalm (89) starts with "I will sing of the Lord's great love forever; with my mouth I will make your faithfulness known through generations."

He knew what He was doing putting those Psalms one after another.

He's okay with us not being okay.

But that's not the end of the story.

His great love and faithfulness is.

~Kelli Bachara, The Unraveling Blog

Crystal Gowen
April 29, 2020 ·

I love this girl!!! She takes snaps and sends them to me.
#graciesnapchat

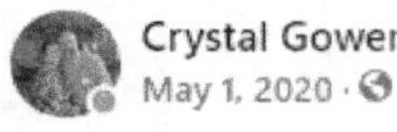

Crystal Gowen
May 1, 2020 ·

It's Brain Tumor Awareness Month!!!! Chronicles of a Brain Tumor Warrior- Crystal's Journey

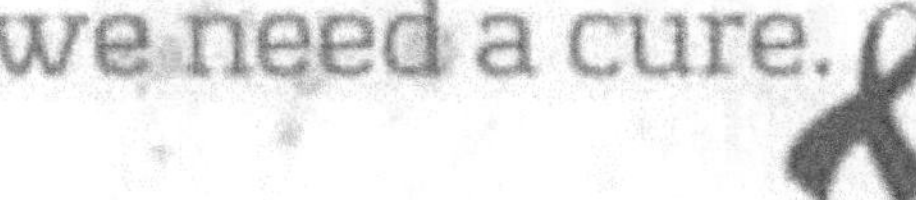

Crystal Gowen
May 1, 2020 ·

Chronicles of a Brain Tumor Warrior- Crystal's Journey

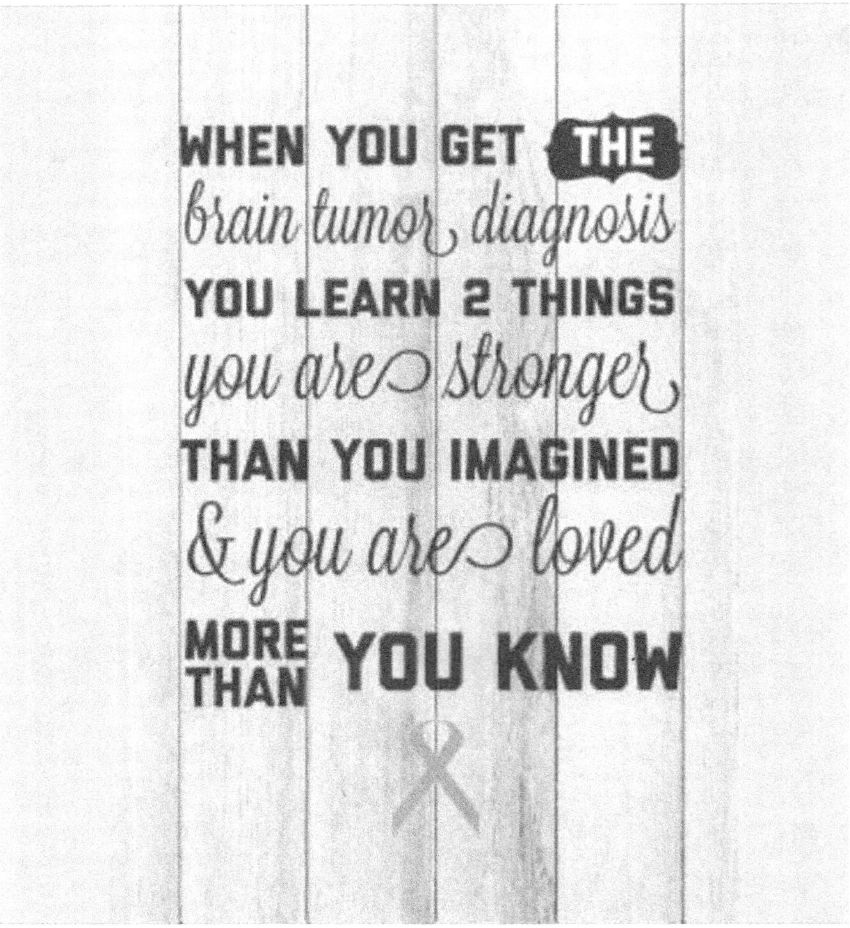

WHEN YOU GET THE
brain tumor diagnosis
YOU LEARN 2 THINGS
you are stronger
THAN YOU IMAGINED
& you are loved
MORE THAN YOU KNOW

Crystal Gowen
May 4, 2020 ·

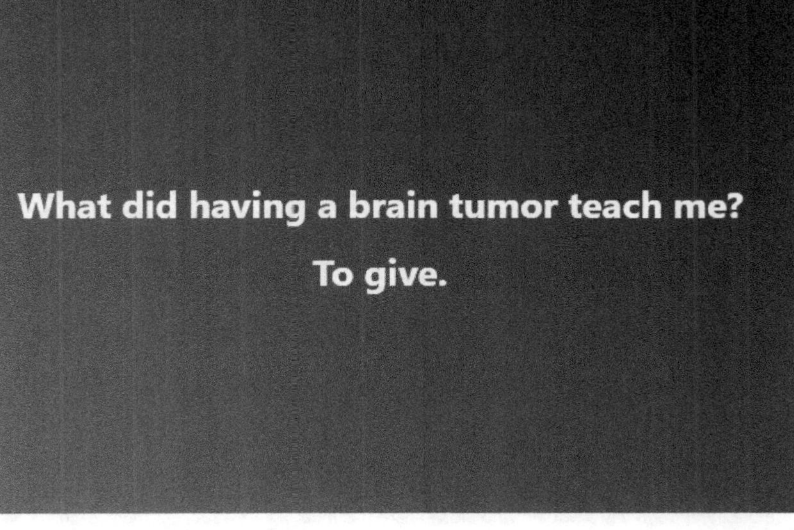

Crystal Gowen is with Lois Edwards.
May 10, 2020 ·

I love this woman with all my heart. She gave birth to a legend...y'all might know her as Connie. Which begot a legacy known as Crystal & Brandie. Her roots are strong and her love is unconditional. She can pull back the raging storm to expose the rainbow admist the sun's glow. She can ease worries with prayers to God and I know she's prayed for me. She is there when I need her and have needed her the most. She has wiped my tears, calmed my fears, and stepped in to care for me as only a mother could through my journey with Ted the Tumor. If I'm half the mother she is, I'll have done something right in this life. I love you Mama more than words can ever say. Happy Mother's Day!!!

Crystal Gowen
June 2, 2020

Chronicles of a Brain Tumor Survivor...

I haven't devoted much time to this as I should. There's not a day that goes by that my journey isn't reflecting its image in my mirror. From its inception on May 28, 2019 until now. It didn't end with surgeries or hospitalizations. It didn't end with PICC lines or medication. It didn't end because God is the author of my story, He has laid out my path and provides direction, and when I feel like I can't tarry onward...He carries me. He lets me sob, get my fears out, and He brings me peace. I can honestly say I'm NOT the same person I used to be. (Lord knows, I hope I'm a better version.)

You might ask how does a journey show its reflection....Well, to tell the truth I can only say when I look at myself I see the battle wound-- Ted left a "Craterville" and some VERY curly hair. Yet, it's more than that. There stands before me a woman who encompasses more love, more compassion, more faith, and more desire to truly be close to my God. In the same breath, there stands a woman who is NOT without struggle, NOT without Satan trying to bring her down or causing havoc, and NOT without sin. There stands a woman who is of the flesh, yet striving for the spirit and grace. The latter is the hardest thing to allow myself. It's part of my journey. Standing before me is definitely a woman who didn't share this much. I've always kept much of this reserved. I've toted a lot of weight as I clung to my baggage...too ashamed to be weak or feel less than before God's eyes. Yet, He knew. My journey has created a woman that delved back into a spirit I locked away many years ago. Yet, God said no more. Ted the Tumor brought that spirit, that joy, that faith back front and center! I found a renewed purpose in my life and while I'm still patiently waiting for God's plan to unfold, I am waiting and listening. I spend my days talking to my family and my work family. Trying to bring humor, love, and peace to whatever the devil throws at us.

I can recall the words of the few people I told prior to announcing my tumor last year. They're etched in my heart. When I read messages, cards, etc (I haven't erased or discarded them) I am brought to tears because of the love and prayers that God heard and the love I needed to get through. God put people in positions in my life then and now to be on this journey with me.

I'm a blessed woman, with a loving husband (who has endured his fair share during this journey), six wonderful children (y'all know blood don't have to make you kin...my bonus babies and bio-babies are my heart), my Daddy & Bonus Mama/Gigi, family and friends that extend across the miles, and my Mama (y'all knew I wasn't gonna leave her out).

I'm blessed to be able to have my Mama (some of y'all know her as Lois, Sister, Mrs. Edwards, Grandma, etc). She's the very best friend and confidant a woman could have because let's face it....nobody writes books or talks about what happens after you turn 30 and don't even think about 40. I think the tell-tell expression I've always heard is "it all goes downhill after 30" or "after your twenties the years just fly by". I concur with the last statement. I was just 20-something, right?!?! Every woman needs a guide, a look-out, somebody to help navigate this route!

She might have forty years on me, but I value every experience she shares, I seek her wisdom, and I treasure her. Her smile and hugs can transport me back to my childhood in a moment. I talk to her every day and if I don't call, you better believe she's calling me to make sure I'm ok. She can read me like an open book. 😊 I'm blessed to be part of her life and her legacy. Thanks to my God for allowing me to share my days with her and those I love!

Lastly, call folks! Talk to them often. Listen to them. Sometimes they need a voice besides the one jibber jabbering in their head. Fortify bonds, create memories, and by all means LOVE.

Chronicles of a Brain Tumor Warrior- Crystal's Journey

Crystal Gowen
June 12, 2020 ·

Super proud of all of our babies!!!
Super duper proud of Nick and his decision to serve our country in the Air Force. He leaves in a couple of months.
Proud of Miss Ashleigh and all of her accomplishments. She's going to do big things in this life.
Proud of Kristin, Nick's girlfriend, on her completion of her associate's degree.
They're amazing!
Two more in middle school!

Crystal Gowen
June 20, 2020 ·

It's my one year crani-anniversary!!!
Thank you God!!!!!
Chronicles of a Brain Tumor Warrior- Crystal's Journey

Crystal Gowen
June 20, 2019 ·

Hey all it's Cameron ! Dr said that her surgery went great and as planned ! Just have to wait to see about her sense of smell . Ted was in there deep but is now evicted !! Thanks to all for the prayers and concerns for the past few days !! Now just to heal from this and keep up the great news !!

Crystal Gowen is with Danny Garris and Gail Garris.
June 21, 2020 ·

Chronicles of a Brain Tumor Survivor...

I've been a Daddy's girl for a long time. There was nothing like being in the shop, before supper, helping my Daddy and just talking while the music played. I'd help with something Daddy was working on and I'd talk about my day as Daddy listened. We've pulled a motor out together, worked on his bike, and sometimes a school project. I went to work with Daddy to earn money at the station. I'd help catch the "front" and pump gas as it was a full service gas station. I'd help Daddy in the bays as I was hoisted up in a car on a lift to "bleed the brakes". I watched my Daddy work out every mechanical problem he was challenged with completing. It might aggravate him, but he never gave up. He seldom missed work...working through colds or when he just didn't feel good. He pushed, gave it his all, and rose each day to do it again. He worked more than forty hours a week, he worked weekends, and was always on call driving the wrecker. He made sure we had what we needed. Always. He always put us first.

I'm forty, a Mom with a house full of teens, and I am in awe of just how my Daddy did it. I know that same work ethic is strong in us. He made sure we were independent minded; could mow grass, change a tire, and operate tools; and depend on ourselves to make a go in it in this world. He taught us boys don't honk horns to pick you up on a date, make-up isn't always necessary, and you don't need a man to take care of you financially. On the flip side, he taught us how a man should love. He endured a lot taking care of Mom. He went through times of trials and tribulations from the time she had kidney cancer to the last days. He did everything he could...giving his all. I'll never forget seeing that same look cross his face when I told him about my brain tumor. He was worried. He came to the hospital and saw me off that morning. Still just as worried, but encouraging me. Yesterday, marked one year since Ted the Tumor was evicted. That morning seeing my Daddy. I wept. I wept because there my Daddy was like always...there for me. He was there for the "me" that was scared, frightened, and anxious. He was there and I'll never forget the hug we shared. It's forever etched in my heart. He was there as they put me to sleep, as I ran through all the faces of just seen. He was there when I woke up. He greeted me with a smile. He has loved me unconditionally. He gave me his last name and I have cherished every moment I have spent with him. This past year has taught me more. Every day I awaken, I turn a new page. I'm thankful God made you my Daddy.

There's nothing like being a Daddy's girl and I would never exchange it for anything.

Happy Father's Day Daddy! You're one in a million.
Chronicles of a Brain Tumor Warrior- Crystal's Journey

Crystal Gowen
July 14, 2020 ·

Crystal Gowen shared a memory.
July 24, 2020 ·

All the glory goes to God! He saved me in more ways than one on this date. He never left me in the troubled waters. He held his palm out and kept me from drowning sorrows, fear, and anxiety. I was in a dark place and He shined His light. From the banks of the shore, he brought me through the storm to the other side. I pray daily He continues to keep those I love covered and well.

3 Years Ago
See your memories >

Crystal Gowen
July 24, 2019 ·

Hello FB it's Cameron here again . I just want everyone to keep Crystal in your thoughts and prayers as she going into surgery at Duke as we speak . Just a minor setback from here previous surgery last month. She was having some swelling in her head due to an infection so Dr is going back in to clean area and make sure there is nothing else going on . Thanks for all the good vibe y'all can send our way!! Brain Tumor Warrior- Crystal's Journey

Crystal Gowen is with **Ashley Cone Kirby** and **Mark Cunningham**.
July 24, 2020 ·

Thank you all for the birthday wishes, texts, and calls.
Chapter 41 was more low key than the medical issues I faced last year. I've come a long way. As I reminisce over the memories I have shared with everyone, I am thankful. God continues to write the chapters of my story...His story and I'm blessed to share it.
As each day passes, we move closer to Mama's official move in date, and that by far seems like one of the best presents God could give me. I'm forever grateful to my BFF Gina Smith who has come to aid us with the move. She's more than my friend, she's a sister and family. Our girls are friends and it warms my heart. In the midst of the moving chaos, I had the opportunity to spend time with my cousin, Belinda Davis, and I recalled lots of mischief. I grin because we weren't all that bad, we just like to nudge the limits. I've had the pleasure to see cousins, even if we are behind masks, and share memories. I've rekindled memories like old movie reels that give a screen play of my life. Days on Belmont Ave. with Grandma and Aunt Daisy, roller skating at Aunt Dot's and Uncle Durwood's, eating lunch with Faye Gardner as she worked, staying with Aunt Barbara Pittman, making peanut butter crackers and homemade marshmallow & crackers, holidays on Downing Street, family reunions, fried chicken and Fort Macon, Sunday dinners at Mama and Papa's, travelling with Aunt Ruby, Mama, and Aunt Dot, time with my Uncle Skinner and being Pearl, Pa Garris' voice and making his grandbabies "ruint", how my babies have changed over the years, and how it all plays into the legacy I'm leaving. I may never fully fathom the imprint I leave upon others or this world daily, but I sure want to leave the legacy of how Jesus has blessed me. As I make new memories, I'm thankful for the people who are in my life...even if we don't talk often, see each other, or even have differing opinions. God's greatest gift is love.

Goodnight!

+46

Crystal Gowen is with **Nickolas Gowen.**
August 30, 2020 ·

Being parents is a tough job.
We pray over our children daily.
It's our job to love them, teach them, gu de them, and let them go when the time is right.
That's our job!

I'm in my feelings y'all.
This young man means the world to me.
We are a blended family.
It takes a lot of hard work, love, and ded cation.
We make it work.
This is what love is!!

He is just as much one of my own as the ones I birthed.
My Mama will tell you that's her great- grandson serving this great country.
He's made a selfless act of courage.
We love him from the bottom up.
Our hearts are full.

John 15:13

Greater love hath no man than this, that a man lay down his life for his friends.

Crystal Gowen
September 4, 2020 ·

I sure do love these babies....
Nickolas Gowen is at BMT (I just keep telling myself it's a really long summer camp.)
In my feelings, I sure do squeeze my other babies a whole lot more.

Crystal Gowen
September 8, 2020 ·

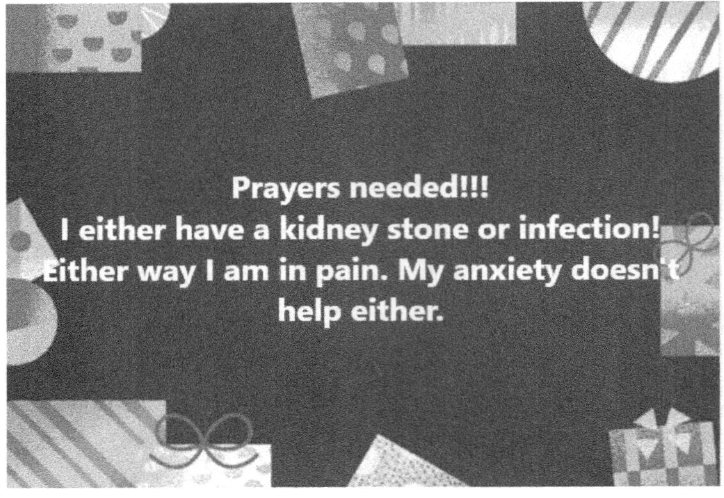

Crystal Gowen
September 13, 2020 ·

Chronicles of a Brain Tumor Survivor

8 days and counting...

It's the annual MRI and Lord knows I have dealt with an increased presence of anxiety. You see anxiety for me has been heightened ever since my Ted journey. The part I have to remember is that God is not taking me back to the journey with this MRI, He's increasing Him and decreasing me. I have to give it to Him. In the past two days, I've imagine being at His feet slowly handing it over and seeing him take it joyfully as a gift that I have trusted Him with. Anxiety is exhausting. The thoughts, the wonder, and the endless duress my soul is in. Most people think I hide it so well, and truthfully I've worked hard to keep it from most of you. Only a few knowing my innermost thoughts, wiping the tears I've shed, and keeping me focused on that mustard seed. Anxiety is difficult to explain...why the thoughts go into this long storyline of what ifs. I have prayed, and continued to pray, to God to take it. Lead me and take the reins. Let it fall from me. Let me have peace. Chronicles of a Brain Tumor Warrior- Crystal's Journey

Jesus and I both know,
that sometimes, I am just
not capable of letting go.
Those are the times when He reminds me
how to lay things down at His feet.
And those are also the times when He
pops my hand like a I'm a toddler,
when I sneak back to pick it up again.
And in those moments,
I've never felt more loved by Him.

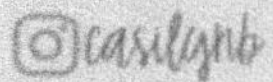

I was told as an undergraduate social work student, this field will burn you out. Social work is a catch-all... you won't just be a social worker because your job will encompass educating, problem-solving, linking, coordinating, filing, scheduling, transporting, etc. You will not be able to change the world, but you can change a spec in time. I think God weighed heavily in my life when he pointed me in this direction. Although there are days, especially in this pandemic, that I have missed lunch, have been stressed, have jumped hoops, have not left my desk even for a potty break because the emails and calls just keep coming and I just need to answer one more, have solved problems non-stop, been faced with life and death situations (I've been in dangerous areas with dangerous people, seen abuse, death, etc.) and have felt like I was burning the midnight oil on both ends of the candle. Yes, I have felt burned out. I have felt like doing something else. Yet, I show up every single day. I push through. I keep going. For what?? For exactly what this says. All of it. There are far more dangerous jobs, yet if there were no social workers, there would be no hope. There would be no change. There would be no impact. The world would be stagnant.

Social workers evoke change. Even just a spec. From listening to others vent to handling matters that bring forth help. God blessed me to be a social worker. It was my calling long before I realized and even on the days I may second guess it, there's a reason he led me to it.

To spread love, hope, and faith---the greatest of all....love. Bringing love to a person, a community, etc. can evoke change. To rise up and advocate for those who do not have a voice, who are feel deterred, or need help.

That's simply why I do it. I give it my all because I am a professional. I take pride in my work and at the end of the day, even through the exhaustion, I help make a difference. In a sense, I may be the answer to prayer someone has prayed to God. Either way, I'm blessed by God to have this career.

Crystal Gowen
September 21, 2020 ·

Welp.....it's about that time.
Cameron has to wait in the Jeep.
And....I have to wear this mask... potentially in my MRI.

Lord,
Please be with me! Let these results be clear!

Chronicles of a Brain Tumor Warrior- Crystal's Journey

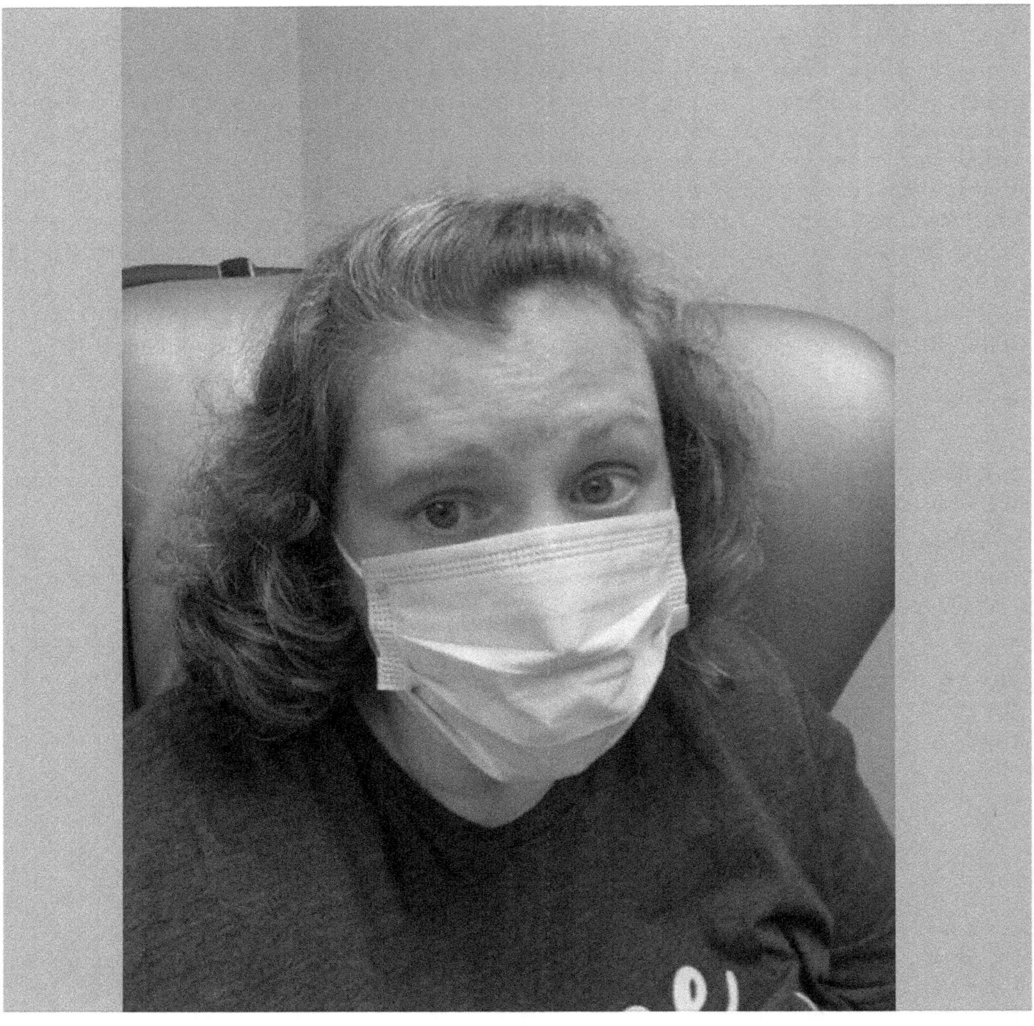

Crystal Gowen
September 22, 2020 ·

MRI was yesterday. Dr. Friedman said the 3x5mm area on my scan yesterday could be a tumor (size of half a pea) or fatty growth. He said nothing to worry about. I go back in a year given its size. If it's clear next year, then every 2 years. Praising my Lord! While it may not say clear, it doesn't say definite. Thank you all for the love and support. I'm praying whatever it is that it's not there next time. More importantly, I pray that my faith continues.

I thank God, with joyful tears, for my family, friends, church, work family, children, and husband, Cameron Gowen. I'm blessed beyond measure. I am proud I was able to have the faith during my MRI- I listened to Christian music and prayed before I entered it- and there was peace. Even though I got the MRI report yesterday afternoon, and I saw the words suspected 3x5 mm meningioma....I knew my God was right there with me. There are days I can't believe God loves me this much....yet my testimony doesn't end. My faith pushed me through even when doubt tried to creep in. Thank you all for being instruments of God.

Chronicles of a Brain Tumor Warrior- Crystal's Journey

Crystal Gowen
October 1, 2020

All of this!!!!
That part about benign tho...
That part about anxiety...
That part about scanxiety...
That part about how much YOU don't feel like you!!!

Today is a hard day, anxiety that doesn't have a reason, but tries to find a root. Can't think of one thing to be anxious about yet the feeling is there. Deep breathes....

Knowing that there is something there and fighting the devil to rid my body of this feeling. Is it scar tissue...is it back??? I know my Savior is working on calming this rooted anxiety that pops up occasionally out of nowhere....where my heart feels like it's beating out of my chest...and there's nothing that has made me anxious all day. It's been a good day. Shew devil!!! Get outta here!
Chronicles of a Brain Tumor Warrior- Crystal's Journey

HAPPYFAMILYHUB.CO.UK

7 things I wish people knew about Brain Tumours - Happy Family Hub

Every year on 1st October, we wear grey to raise awareness of the often invisible illness of brai...

Crystal Gowen
October 27, 2020

Chronicles of a Brain Tumor Survivor...

O Lord, thank you for my blessings. Life has been somewhat busy and I've taken my eyes off of you for a moment, yet you continue to bless me. Reminding me of all that I'm thankful. Thank you for my husband, my Mama, my children, the support of family, friends, and an amazing staff. They keep me grounded in you Lord. Sometimes I can't see the forest for trees, yet you never fail me. You see the very best of my heart and you never desert my soul. You lay things on my heart that most others won't understand because it's Your will for the greater good of those I love and who love me. Lord willing may you give me strength to tarry onward through all things. Chronicles of a Brain Tumor Warrior- Crystal's Journey

Crystal Gowen
December 6, 2020 ·

Me: Can you take my place for the Toy Run?
Gracie: Absolutelllly....

She's all layered up taking my place on today's run. She picked out two toys, one for a girl and one for a boy. Thanks baby girl for stand ng in for me. Have a great time with Dad.

@gowen_gracie
@mopar__bigred_79
Chronicles of a Brain Tumor Warrior- Crystal's Journey

Crystal Gowen
December 16, 2020 ·

I'm thankful for this Christmas season. Yet another year has passed and I'm even more grateful than the last. I know I'm more blessed than ever as I'm here. Ted the Tumor didn't take me out. The Lord said "no weapon formed against me shall prosper" and the Lord has kept that promise all my life, even when I strayed from Him. I can't lie and say this year has been easy. It's been very difficult for all of us in various ways. Seems like we face more setbacks at every turn, but God is always ready with a comeback. #nottodaysatan
Chronicles of a Brain Tumor Warrior- Crystal's Journey

Crystal Gowen
December 25, 2020

On this Christmas, I'm reminded of the faith I have. The God I serve blessed this world with a baby in a manger to save us from sin. I know I fail him daily, but the mercy and grace God has shown me far outweigh anything the devil can throw at me. John 3:16 is the very first Bible verse I ever learned. Psalm 91 is the verse that brought me through the most difficult time. I've learned you don't have to be a scholar to be a Christian...only a believer that never loses what God has given us....faith, hope, and love. In a manger so long ago, these three things were a swaddled baby lying in the manger who grew to die for our sins and be resurrected in three days. God Almighty is good today, tomorrow, and all the time! The devil may have 20-20ed us, but the good Lord will always protect and provide.

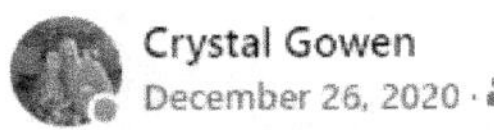
Crystal Gowen
December 26, 2020

The best Christmas gift arrived in a manger full of love and hope. Y'all I prayed we would be able to see Nickolas Gowen this Christmas even though we were told otherwise (all part of his surprise). God answers prayers. I'm sure many of you have seen the videos Nick's mom, Beth Medlin, and I put up. Just know going into 2021, you can always end a bad year full of a pandemic on a blessing. God blessed our entire family with Nick's presence. And yes, our entire family truly includes our side, his mom's side, and Kristin's side. We are forever blended, etched in stone, built by love, and faithful for the blessings bestowed. We've moved mountains to make it happen and we tarry through obstacles on this journey for all of our babies. As the years pass by, our children become grown, we will always, always, always want the joy in our children's hearts to be as memorable as this occasion. If you have a blended family, work at it always!!!! God Bless!

Crystal Gowen
December 31, 2020

Chronicles of a Brain Tumor Survivor...

It's the end of 2020. I've survived another year. Not totally unscathed, but blessed nonetheless. January- Brought in a new year and post holiday bustle. We returned back to our everyday hustle.

February- We shared Valentine's and prepared for Nick and Ashleigh's senior year.

March-Now- Global pandemic, survived COVID-19, celebrated birthdays and holidays way different than before, masks and 6 ft apart are daily life, I'm working from home, the kids are homeschooled, the eldest kids had a drive thru graduation, Nick left for the Air Force, church attendance was via Facebook or at Mama's where we drove and remained in our cars, there was a scramble for toilet paper and cleaning supplies, I Skyped with my friends (I've not seen Jen since January or Feb face-to-face), I had an MRI (there's a half-pea sized something up thete- praying it's scar tissue), another dent in my forehead has settled, work is harder as we help people cope with the very reality we are all facing. Yet, God has blessed us through every single situation. He has kept us covered and protected. As I enter, 2021 (geez I never did phanthom these decades-- I was just trying to survive the 90s and early 00s), I look forward to the future: Kristin and Nick are engaged, Mama is healthy, Cam continues to provide for us all as our family leader, and the kids are doing well. I pray in 2021 I continue to walk closer to God, I spend time with my family as best as I can (phone calls, video chats), I strive to help others in my job, and I grow as a person!

Chronicles of a Brain Tumor Warrior- Crystal's Journey

Chronicles of a Brain Tumor Survivor....

So this week, I've had to ask God to calm my seas. As of late, there's so much going on and anxiety had crept up. God sent His peop e to help me. I'm dealing with a skin infection. Well...that's not serious you think, but it's on my forehead. Sound the alarms!!!! Yeah that's how I've been feeling, but after much and I do mean a lot of prayer, my Mama praying over it, my husband reassuring me, my children giving me hugs, and my best friends from high school providing much encouragement and support...God has calmed the seas that anxiety torments. Yet, through this setback, it was pointed out that I have to give myself grace as I felt disappointed for not having more faith than I did and letting the anxiety jostle me about. I'm much harder on myself these days than I presume God is when it comes to my faith. I want to be all I can be for God. In doing so, I have to give myself some grace, some self-compassion, and as I was told God never leaves you. The skin infection is healing. I return in one week claiming that it will be healed.
Chronicles of a Brain Tumor Warrior- Crystal's Journey

I had nothing to bring Him but my broken heart, yet He gave me everything!

Crystal Gowen
January 28, 2021 ·

And bangs.....

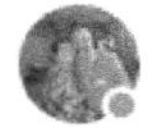

Crystal Gowen is at Wilson Dermatology.
March 23, 2021 · Wilson ·

Lord,

Let this thing be insignificant.

Amen

Crystal Gowen
March 23, 2021 ·

Well y'all....it's not the outcome I have wanted for this "dent" in my forehead. I'm back at Duke. Dr. Friedman is checking me out for possible bone infection. I'm waiting to do a CT scan. I've had labs taken. Once I'm done, I'll return home until he calls. Please pray for me. Chronicles of a Brain Tumor Warrior- Crystal's Journey

Crystal Gowen
March 24, 2021 ·

"Behold, the LORD'S hand is not shortened, that it cannot save; neither his ear heavy, that it cannot hear:"
Isaiah 59:1, KJV

"I cried unto the LORD with my voice, and he heard me out of his holy hill. Selah."
Psalm 3:4, KJV

"For I said in my haste, I am cut off from before thine eyes: nevertheless thou heardest the voice of my supplications when I cried unto thee."
Psalm 31:22, KJV

"I sought the LORD, and he heard me, and delivered me from all my fears."
Psalm 34:4, KJV

"I cried unto God with my voice, even unto God with my voice; and he gave ear unto me."
Psalm 77:1, KJV

"In my distress I cried unto the LORD, and he heard me."
Psalm 120:1, KJV

I have cried, shed a many a tear throughout yesterday, the night, and this morning. Cried out to God. I'd be lying if I said a mess. The CT scan results are in, but I'm waiting on the doctor to tell me what's next. I know I shouldn't worry, but it's so much easier than done. Chronicles of a Brain Tumor Warrior- Crystal's Journey

Crystal Gowen
March 24, 2021 ·

Duke is waiting on the culture results taken at my appointment yesterday in Wilson. They will call me and let me know what the plan will be. Praying the erosion of my bone flap is not due to an infection. The PA stated the ct scan showed that it may NOT due to infection. I'm going to claim this in my God's name! I'm standing on his promises y'all! I'm praying that culture is negative. I'm praying that this will be ok and no matter what I am His!!! I am His daughter. When I cry out He hears my prayers! Chronicles of a Brain Tumor Warrior- Crystal's Journey

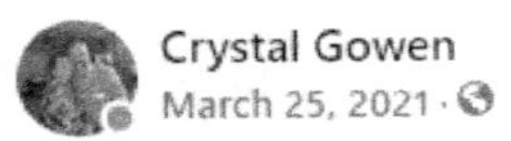

Crystal Gowen
March 25, 2021 ·

Y'all! I'm still on the waiting end of things, BUT I'm standing on God's promises. The preliminary report indicates no growth. I know this can change because cultures take time, but I'm claiming no growth!!!! No infection! Please continue to pray for peace, patience, and no growth! The Lord brought me peace yesterday evening. He brought me calmness to the devil's storm. Not today Satan!!! Not today! I'm claiming my prayers and yours will be heard! My Father sent his only begotten SON for moments just like this.... To draw me nearer, closer, and within the closeness of God. I am blessed with SO many people that have called, texted, visited, prayed, sang to me, and shared songs. You're a blessing in my life and the sign the Holy Spirit is here with me and shielding me. Lift your hands up!!!! I know that there's something going on from blood work, but I know my God can heal me from head to toe! Chronicles of a Brain Tumor Warrior- Crystal's Journey

Crystal Gowen
March 26, 2021 ·

Tom Petty always said the waiting is the hardest part, BUT God said to be still and know that I AM GOD. Let me tell you about my God today....
Neurosurgeon's office calls to tell me so far no infectious bacteria has grown, only some evidence of skin flora (that natural stuff on my face). Claiming it y'all!!!
He did tell me that the bone flap erosion could be attributed to they put it back together, just not as good as the good Lord did when he made me. So.... We wait.
I'm waiting on a call, likely Monday, to tell me what the plan is. So, God is telling me to be still.
Thank y'all for the outpouring of love. Prayers work. I'm claiming the prayers I ask for, you ask for, my family asks for, my church family asks for will be answered if it's God's will. Chronicles of a Brain Tumor Warrior- Crystal's Journey

YOUTUBE.COM
Hillary Scott & The Scott Family - Still (Lyric Video)
Purchase Hillary Scott's Grammy Award winning album LOVE REMAINS: http://umgn.us/hillary...

Crystal Gowen
March 28, 2021 ·

Chronicles of a Brain Tumor Survivor...
Well, it's chapter four to this journey. Ted the Tumor was evicted in June 2019. The infection was removed July 2019 (my 40th birthday to be exact). The PICC line meds left me neutropenic. Now... There's a dent in my forehead where it's obvious in the CT scan the bone has eroded. I don't know what that means yet. I'm holding onto my faith with white knuckles. Just praying and trying not to pick this weight back up. It's so hard when the depression and anxiety wage a war. The two main things Ted left me with that I have worked so hard to push through. The desire to want to "plan" for something can be overwhelming at times...to be prepared. Sure, I've experienced these issues before, but y'all after Ted this is an entirely different level. I have had a good weekend by far and when my thoughts linger too long on this...I push forward and remember....

By myself
It won't work
Lord I need
I need Your help
By myself
It won't work
Lord I need
I need Your help

I'm hoping we find answers tomorrow that resolve the place on my forehead and the dent, too.
Chronicles of a Brain Tumor Warrior- Crystal's Journey

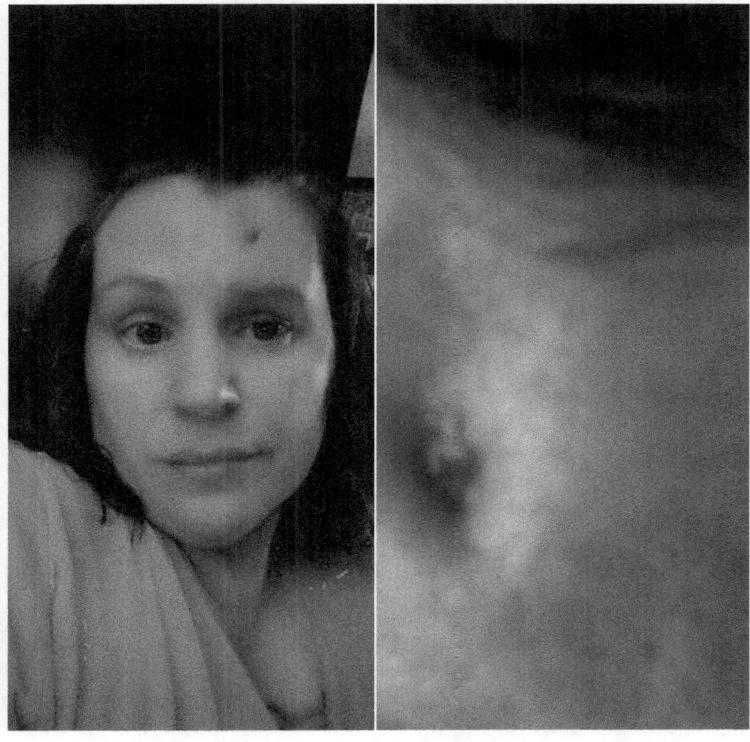

Chronicles of a Brain Tumor Survivor...

I have a referral to a plastic surgeon for further consult. Dr. Friedman is suspicious this is due to chronic osteomyelitis of my bone flap, along with the findings of the CT scan of the bone's erosion. In conjunction with the consult, it is probable the bone flap will be removed and replaced with titanium or plastic. More to come on that later. So.....there's a campaign to remove Dana the Dent and her brother, Oscar Osteomyelitis. If we remove the bone flap, then the chronic osteomyelitis will be resolved. I thank God for every prayer said on my behalf. Please continue to pray. #byedanathedent #toodlesoscar Chronicles of a Brain Tumor Warrior- Crystal's Journey

Thank you everyone for the prayers. Dr. Erdmann said he will need to complete twc surgeries. The bone area is necrotic and will need to be removed. The titanium plate will be replaced 3-6 months later. Without a bone flap to protect my skull, I will need to wear a helmet. Surgery will be in April. The date has not been scheduled yet. This is a lot for me to process. Having the possibility of no forehead or partial forehead (they will need to examine the other side once they get in there) removal is a lot. Prayers appreciated. Chronicles cf a Brain Tumor Warrior- Crystal's Journey

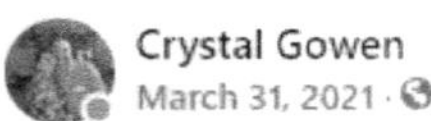

Thank you all for the prayers, calls, texts, and music you have brightened my life with at this moment. Today, has been a lot. That's all I can come up with....just a lot. I'm facing one surgery that will have me disfigured, while the other will hopefully bring me back to something better. The unknown is the hardest part. As a woman, not knowing what I will look like after the first surgery to the last surgery will have to be something I will have to overcome, BUT God is good. No matter what I know HE will provide. Chronicles of a Brain Tumor Warrior- Crystal's Journey

Chronicles of a Brain Tumor Survivor...

I've decided to spend my remaining days until surgery serving God the best way I can and casting my fears at his feet. Chronicles of a Brain Tumor Warrior- Crystal's Journey

Crystal Gowen
April 30, 2021 ·

Pics from yesterday.... Chronicles of a Brain Tumor Warrior- Crystal's Journey

Crystal Gowen
April 30, 2021 ·

Good Morning Facebook!!!!!! Ain't God good?!?! I'm out of surgery and all went well. Waiting for the doctors to make their rounds, but they only had to take a small portion and not the entire forehead. I'm in awe. This morning I met a woman having surgery, as you know you have to be dropped off and be by yourself, but we witnessed and talked about our Lord and Savior!!!! My God is SO good!!! I am thankful and blessed for all of the prayers said over me, for me, and for those working with me. God is amazing!!! Y'all get ready for a testimony!!!! Chronicles of a Brain Tumor Warrior- Crystal's Journey

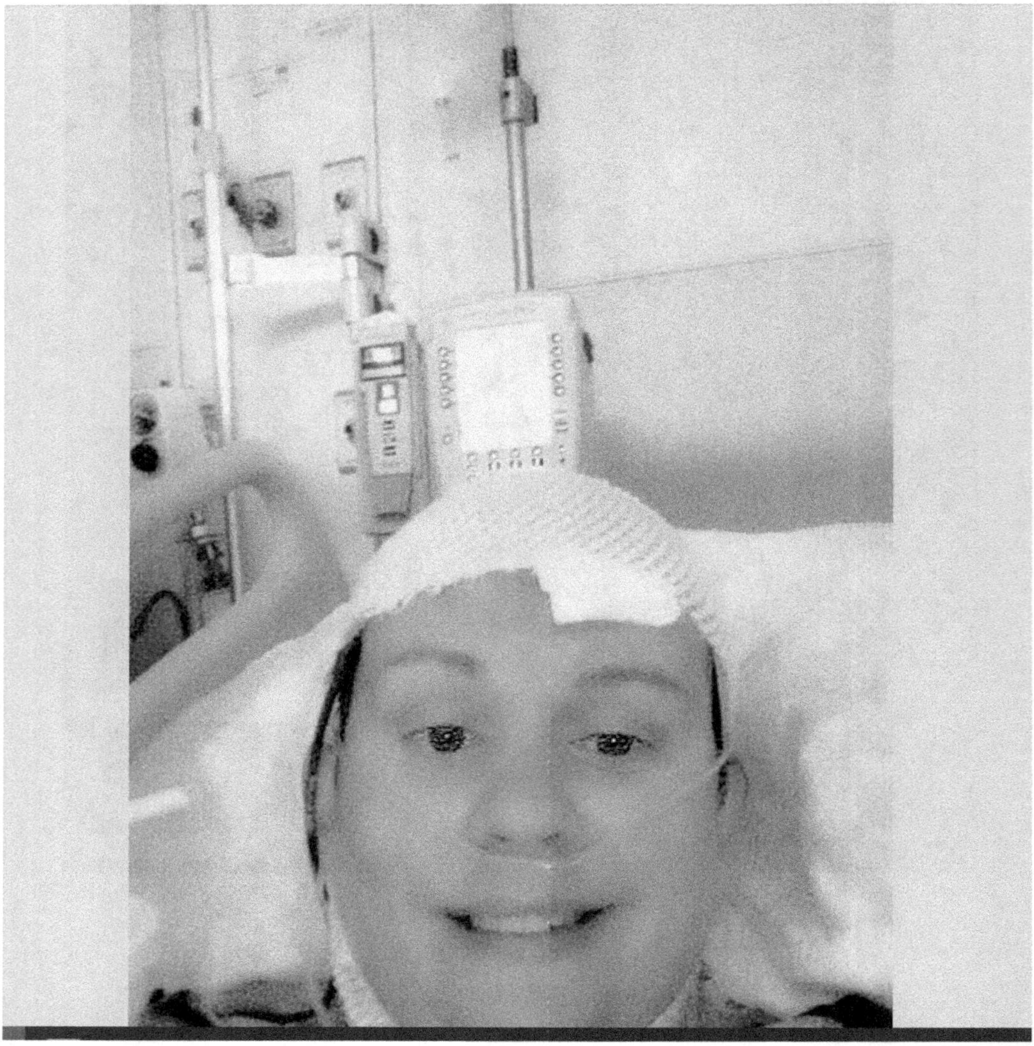

Crystal Gowen
May 2, 2021 ·

Relying on God's grace, faith, and hope for the days ahead. Trusting in his promises and timing.

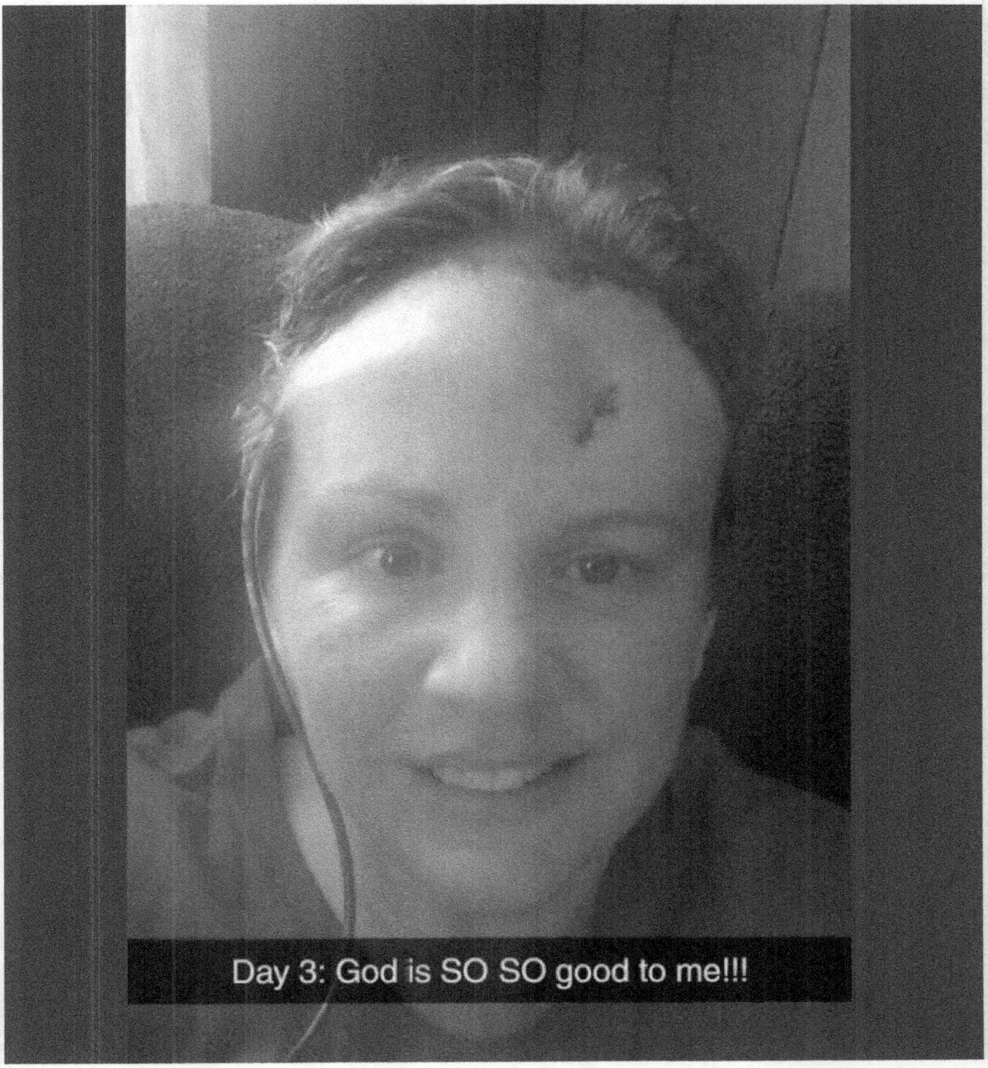

Day 3: God is SO SO good to me!!!

Crystal Gowen

May 3, 2021 ·

Day 4....

Pseudomonas is my nemesis again! Continue to stay the course on the antibiotics they discharged me with. Little more sore, tired, and ready for the drain tube to finish up. But seriously, I'm taking it one day at a time. Chronicles of a Brain Tumor Warrior- Crystal's Journey

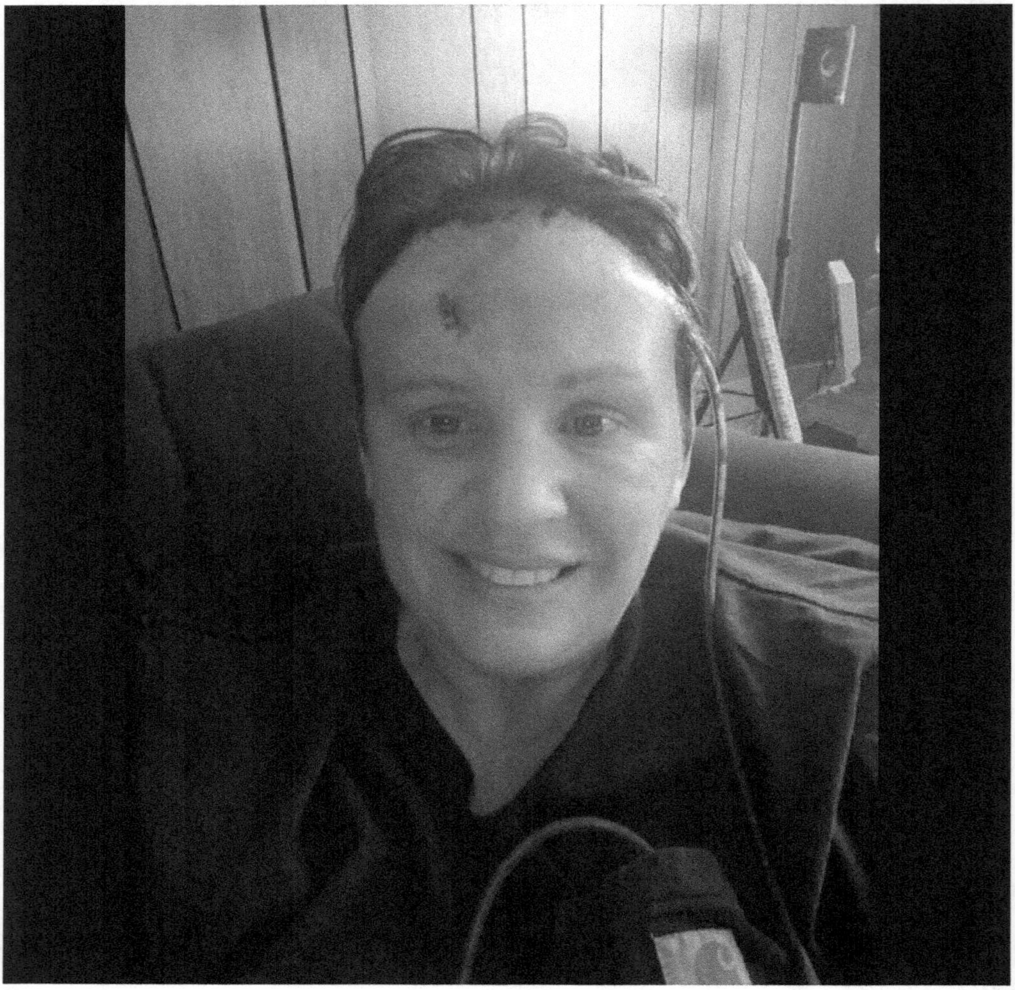

Crystal Gowen
May 4, 2021 · YouTube ·

I have felt God's spirit SO much more this time. The journey is still hard because there are medical unknowns. There always are, yet I KNOW HE has all the answers. I am trusting in His timing and His spirit.n Chronicles of a Brain Tumor Warrior- Crystal's Journey

YOUTUBE.COM

Tasha Cobbs Leonard - Your Spirit ft. Kierra Sheard (Official Video)

Official Music Video for "Your Spirit" by Tasha Cobbs Leonard ft. Kierra Sheard taken from the ...

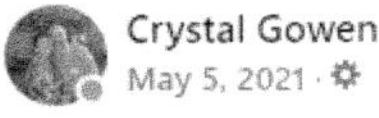

Crystal Gowen
May 5, 2021 ·

Jesus,

I look at this scar riddled head and think about how they don't compare to the pain You endured and the scars left behind. The ultimate scar of sin you assumed because You didn't want to be without us. I accept these scars graciously as part of my journey.

Amen

Chronicles of a Brain Tumor Warrior- Crystal's Journey

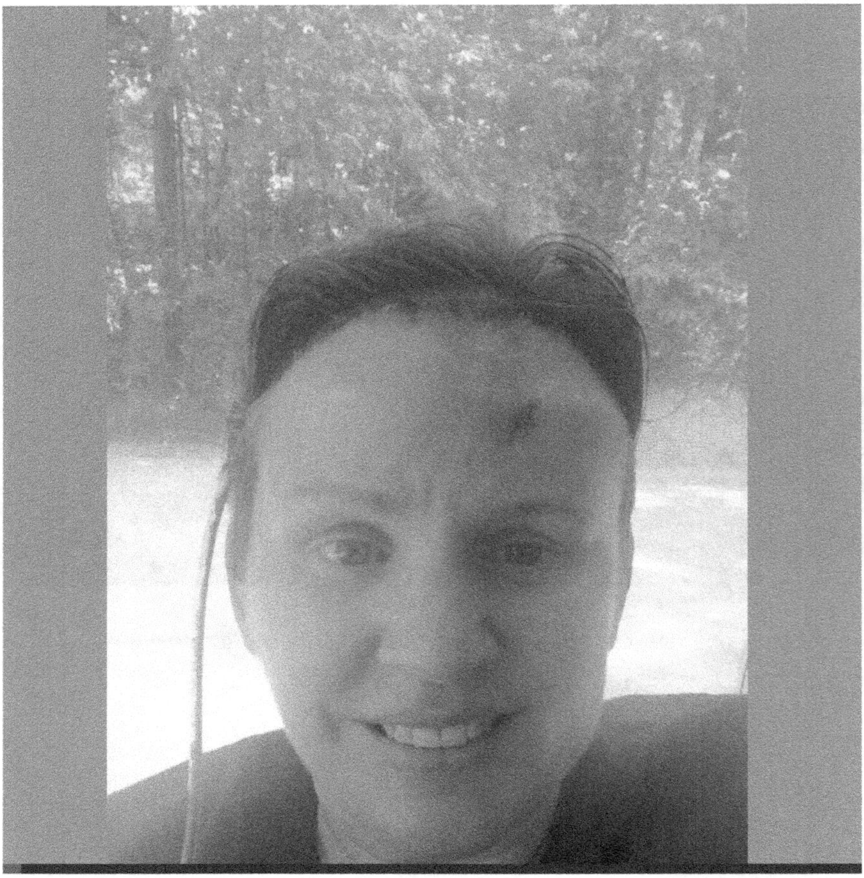

Crystal Gowen
May 6, 2021 ·

I don't hide my scars. They are proof that I showed up for life. And fought.

unknown

wordables.

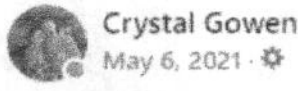

Crystal Gowen
May 6, 2021 ·

I sure hope my story....scratch that....my testimony will help someone

One day you will
tell your story
of how you overcame
what you went through
and it will be
someone else's
survival guide.

BRENE BROWN

Goalcast

Crystal Gowen
May 8, 2021 ·

Praising my God in the midst of this storm!
Ain't nothing like that Holy Water!
I don't own the rights to music.
Chronicles of a Brain Tumor Warrior- Crystal's Journey

Crystal Gowen
May 9, 2021 ·

Keep the chill off my head.... Thankful for the nurses who donated their caps to the cancer center at Duke. This one has been a life saver for going out. Keeps the sun from burning me and the cold from bothering me. Chronicles of a Brain Tumor Warrior- Crystal's Journey

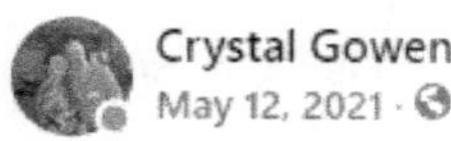

Crystal Gowen
May 12, 2021 ·

Good God Almighty!!!! Praise the Lord!! Jesus, You have done it again!!!! The drain is removed! All is going well! Adding an antibiotic for the culture that came back -- DIE Pseudomonas DIE in Jesus name-- and returning next week to remove sutures. Dr. Erdmann stated he removed a small portion of infected bone. The rest of the flap is vital. Jesus heard my prayers! He removed hardware from the same side. No second surgery is necessary!!!! Yes Jesus!!!! I am just overjoyed with praise and love for my Lord!!! I was annoited and prayed over by SO many prior to my surgery. In that prayer, specially prayed over me the Sunday before, we asked God to take it away and at that time it was the need for the bone flap to be removed and a second surgery to include a titanium plate. Y'all!!!! Jesus heard our prayers and took that away. So much less was needed! I awoke from surgery praising my God and I won't stop.... There's a story he wants told....a testimony shared. I SO appreciate the prayers, love, and everything everyone has and continues to do to help my family. 💜 Chronicles of a Brain Tumor Warrior- Crystal's Journey

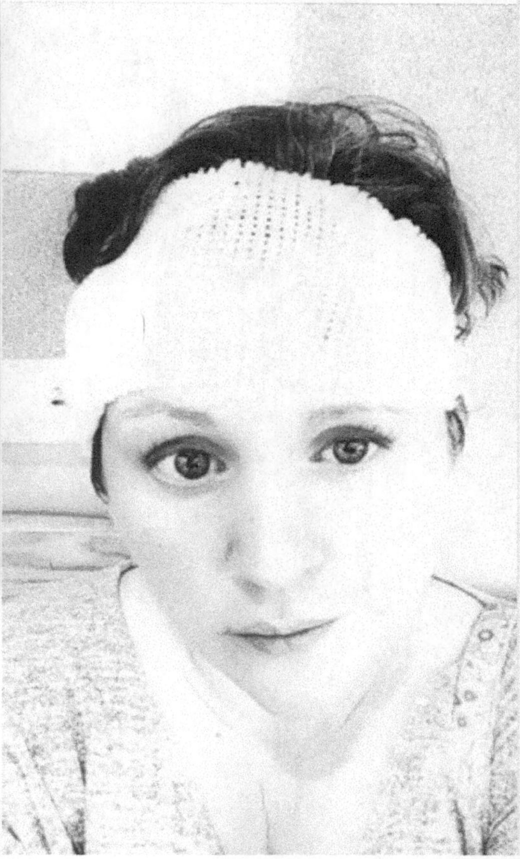

Crystal Gowen
May 13, 2021 ·

Just some swelling after JP drain removal.....

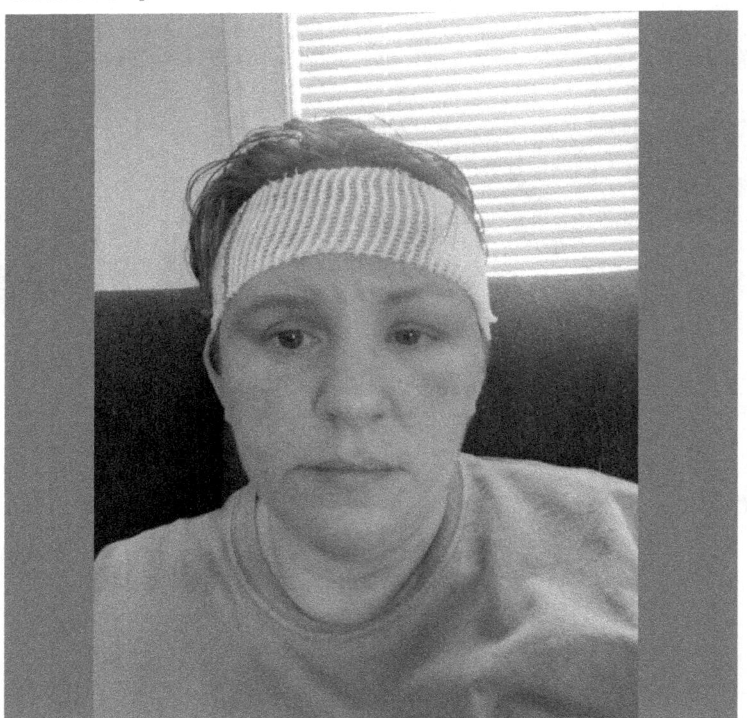

Crystal Gowen
May 13, 2021 ·

Welp.....I'm swelling near my eye only. Ugh!!!!

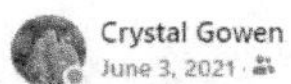

Crystal Gowen
June 3, 2021 ·

Day 1: Let's try this recovery thing again. I'm home to make sure I take care of myself until July 1. I'll be following physician orders, so being back to work has been postponed until then. 😞 Please keep us in your prayers.

Crystal Gowen
June 7, 2021 ·

My Dearest Cameron,

If we were given multiple lifetimes, I'd spend them all with you.
The way you look across a room or with my face cupped in your loving hands.
I remember our first kiss under a country moon and stars.
I remember every hand holding moment as we strolled those school hallways.
How you'd tuck me in the corner in hopes no one would see the kiss you caressed my lips with before we departed to class.
I remember those kids and that blossoming love.

That love that remained through separation of years, picking up the pen to write more pages to this love story, trials and tribulations, and enormous blessings.
It's the legacy of all that we were and the foundation throughout our years.
It's the smiles, the embraces, the laughter, and the tears.
It's the connection that can't be broken by space, time, or obstacles.
It endures.

It pours readily from us.
Fulfilling the pages of our story.

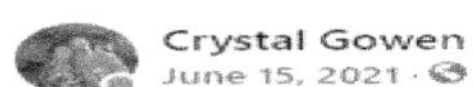

Crystal Gowen
June 15, 2021 ·

Sooooooo I went for a trim. It was getting HAWT!!!! Pulled my hair back with a headband and my little bangs are coming in... Chronicles of a Brain Tumor Warrior- Crystal's Journey

Crystal Gowen is at **Duke Health (Duke Clinic).**
June 30, 2021 · Durham ·

Let's see what this lump is on my forehead.

Crystal Gowen
June 30, 2021 ·

Thank you Lord!!! That lump is just my lymphatic system being slow. Massage and keep an eye on it. PTL!!! Chronicles of a Brain Tumor Warrior- Crystal's Journey

Crystal Gowen shared a memory.
July 24, 2021 ·

Today marks another year I am blessed by God to celebrate my existence. I am thankful for all that He has blessed me with and hopeful for many more. At 10:03 a.m. my Mom brought me into this world. I'm only saddened by the fact that she's not here to celebrate with me, but just maybe she's blowing out candles for me in Heaven. I 💙 you Mom and more than any words could have ever expressed I'm so very thankful for you.

4 Years Ago
See your memories >

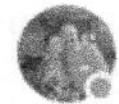

Crystal Gowen
July 24, 2018 ·

To the woman who gave birth to legends...Mom.
As much as I'm celebrated today...I give the credit all to you for making a choice to give life.
So much life has occurred since these pictures, but most importantly its a life created and filled with hope, love, and faith. It's not perfect. It's been full of laughter, joy, sadness, defeat, accomplishments, success, determination, people...oh the people who are blessings to me!!!!
My tears may fall...but my soul knows you're just waiting for me, so we can pick up right where we left off. Love you Mom.

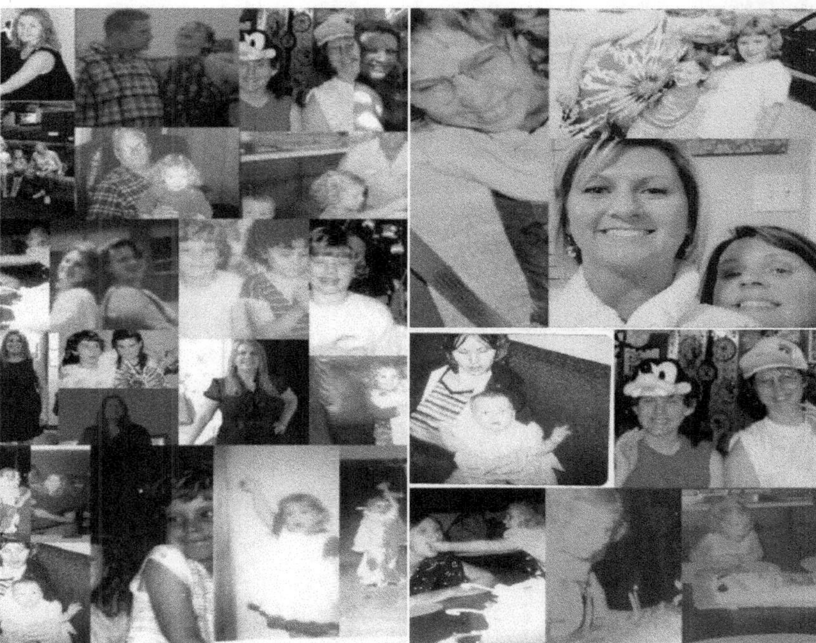

Crystal Gowen
September 19, 2021 ·

Tuesday is the day.
I am praying for myself to:

Show my adoration for God. He is the Almighty, the alpha & the omega, the beginning and the end. He is wonderful, beautiful, holy. He is everything I seek. He is love, hope, and faith. He is just. He is fair. He is loving.

To Confess- Yes confess. Confess I am flesh and in that flesh I am not perfect. I ask to forgive all my sins and to forgive any trespasses I have amongst others as I forgive them. I ask to cleanse me for every moment I fall short in the glory of the Lord.

Show Thanksgiving- Lord!!! Without you I am nothing. I am thankful for all that God has done for me. Just His Mighty presence in my life. He has never left me and during the trials and tribulations I have grown. He has put blessing after blessing in my life from people, opportunities, connections, and the grandiose beauty of the world he created and all people and things that are in it. I am in awe 24/7.

And finally supplication- I am here Lord. I am faithfully awaiting your answer Dear Lord. I know I have to move forward, cast away my fears, and know that no matter what You are GOD Almighty. If it is your will give me the answer, as you do each year. You will not forsake me and Lord, I just ask you for peace, calmness, and to listen and not to be afraid.

Scanxiety is real. This is the first year I can confess and say I am better than I was the year before. Yet, I know each time I prepare for a scan, I have to be calm. I have to wait. I have to know it is in Your time, and not my own.

Please pray for me as I prepare not only physically, but mentally.

God Bless FB Family!
Chronicles of a Brain Tumor Warrior- Crystal's Journey

Crystal Gowen is at Duke Cancer Center.
September 21, 2021 · Durham ·

Arrived...
Parked...
Time to check in.
MRI & MD appointment to follow.
Lord if it's your will, let me be blessed with good results.

Crystal Gowen
September 21, 2021 ·

Tonight.....
How this resonates. I just want Connie to make it better. To go to the ends of the Earth, cuss and bust heads, help me pick myself up. Don't get me wrong, I got Mama, but I wished I had Mom, too. To fill that void.

HAPPINESS, HOPE & HARSH REALITIES

The day she dies, you become an adult.

The kind of adult that doesn't have a mother. That is a different kind of adult than before. ***Trust me.***

xox Chelsea Ohlemiller

Crystal Gowen

September 21, 2021 ·

I have a reoccurring tumor near the same area. It's not the news I wanted, but God is writing my story. It's a time for growth and testimony.

It's time to believe for the impossible.
Speak to the mountain and tell it to move. By your stripes I am healed. You said it, I believe it. You said it, it is done. Move the immovable. Break the unbreakable. God we believe. God we believe for it. We will see a miracle.
-CeCe Winans

Chronicles of a Brain Tumor Warrior- Crystal's Journey

YOUTUBE.COM

CeCe Winans - Believe For It (Acoustic One Take)

Hear the acoustic one take session of CeCe's new song "Believe For It"Stream the song & pre-...

Chronicles of a Brain Tumor....
Well, I've survived one. Let's strap our boots up and deal with the next one. That's what I tell myself every. single. day. Yet, there's a place that seeps to the surface--- I am overwhelmed with thoughts of what I have experienced and thoughts of what is yet to come. I have a bottle of emotions....like they're playing tug of war and I'm in the middle. The fear, sadness, and weariness gets to me some days. Then I think if we remove this one...will another come back? What is my quality of life going to be like? How will it affect my children? My parents? My Mama? My husband? How exhausting a thought.
I struggle, but I lace up my boots and try to give it all to each day. I want to experience the best of the best and enjoy them all. Not take them for granted. So much loss has occurred around us. It takes its toll and reminds me just how precious life is. I know I have a beautiful place to look forward to in the arms of my Jesus and it gives me comfort for the day He calls me home. Hoping He keeps me here to see my first grandbaby, my kids finish school, my kids reach milestones, and to share the days with my husband. I trust in his plan so much....but those emotions are raw and they're harder some days than others.
So, here's to the chronicles of a brain tumor.... here's to reaching the survivor status again. Not sure what to call her---she's pretty dainty--- "Tempie", "Tatiana", "Olga" (olfactory groove)-- but she's going to kick rocks too! 'Til then Tumor! ✌ Chronicles of a Brain Tumor Warrior- Crystal's Journey

Crystal Gowen
October 31, 2021 ·

When every imperfection inspires you to be who God commands you to be. Chronicles of a Brain Tumor Warrior- Crystal's Journey

Crystal Gowen
December 24, 2021 ·

The BEST Christmas gift I got this year was time. Not the kind of time you keep up with using a watch, but genuine time. Yesterday, I helped my Aunt Selma (91) and my Mama (almost 83) celebrate their niece, Faye's, 75th birthday. It's the time when you BLESS reckless drivers on back roads, wait an hour to eat at a restaurant in the middle of nowhere, shop while you wait and watch the three of them engineer a bird house project for Mama. It's the road trip you couldn't imagine when you were a youngin, but it's the one you crave and need as an adult. We ended the trip visiting Aunt Thelma (91). You can see two aunts helping their niece and they all would do for one another hands down. Aunt Thelma greeted me with the biggest hug and I smiled more genuinely being among those strong women in my family. They say strength comes in numbers. I say strength comes from love. Those women love beyond time, the depths of darkness, and the light of day. It's that TIME that I seek in my life.

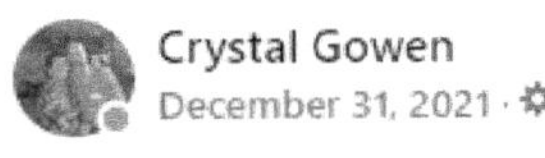

Crystal Gowen
December 31, 2021 ·

2021,

You've taken a lot out of/from me, my family, my friends, and my work family. There have truly been some hard days, some inexplicable days, and some dark ones. We have tarried on through it all. I won't let this year end on a bad note because you have given me these memories forever etched in my heart.

Cheers 2021

Another page added to my story.

Here's to 2022!

+18

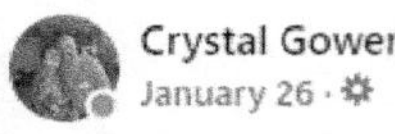

Crystal Gowen
January 26 ·

En route to Duke today and I always look for the same reminders. The industrial areas, the areas of town that haven't blossomed in the past twenty years, and the new skyline of edgy growth casting shadows over all of it.
How many times have I made this drive? Looked at these same things? Prayed the same prayers? It's a story I have written so many pages on. Having the ability to write a page means God continues my story. There is breathe in each page.
Recently, I watched the casket close when my Aunt Peggy died and I thought there are no more pages to be written. No breathe to be felt, warmth to be sought in hugs. Yet, I realize there is a story to read from. Sometimes God writes not for us to fill pages, but for us to read them.
I'm reading pages this morning. Chronicles of a Brain Tumor Warrior- Crystal's Journey

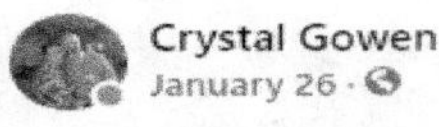

Crystal Gowen
January 26 ·

3-D craniofacial CT scan scheduled for Monday. More news to come, but the impression is it could be more bone failure due to infection stemming from the infection in 2019. However, God is writing this story and the finale to this chapter isn't ready for release. So, we wait.

Thank you SO much for your prayers and love. They always mean so much to me. The texts and calls always bring joy deep down to my soul. Chronicles of a Brain Tumor Warrior- Crystal's Journey

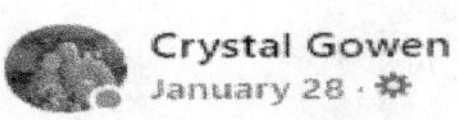

Crystal Gowen
January 28 ·

One of my takeaways from my doctor's appointment was - "You're overworked and you need to take care of yourself." He didn't ask me my opinion, he gave me his medical opinion.
For the past few days, I have prayed and prayed for a solution to find the balance. Working from home is not a piece of cake. The field I work is hard and burnout is real. I'm in year #22. It's been a lot of giving of myself, especially the past few years as our system endures revolutionary changes toppled by a pandemic that has not only brought so many deaths, but so much hardship on healthcare and behavioral health care. Folks, we ARE not ok.
Yet, I have realized the words of my surgeon, I have to take care of myself for the best outcome. That means I cannot keep repeating treating my acute problem, but I have to address the big picture. I'm praying for answers because a balance is what I need. In the words of Sam Cooke- A Change is Gonna Come. Chronicles of a Brain Tumor Warrior- Crystal's Journey

Crystal Gowen
January 29 ·

Cropped/Pinned Look....
&
Those natural curls...

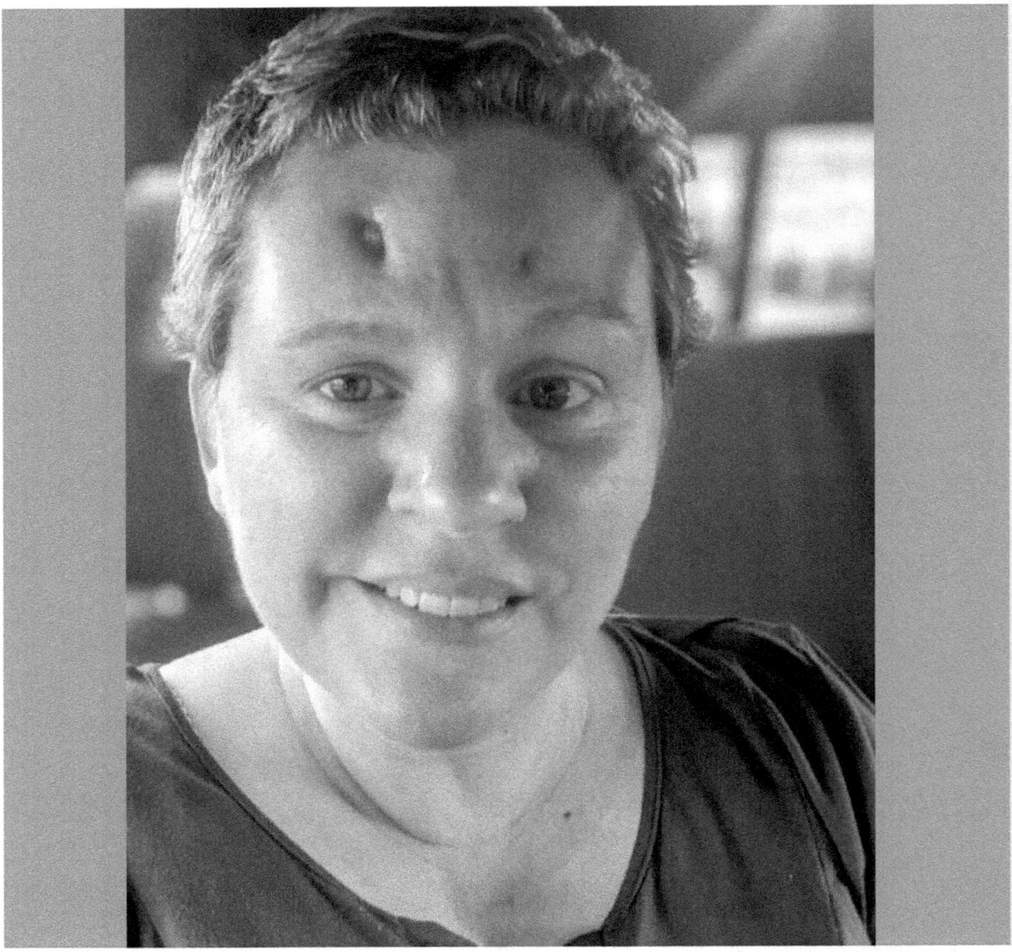

Crystal Gowen is at **Duke Raleigh Hospital Outpatient Imaging Center.**
January 31 · Raleigh ·

Here we go....

Crystal Gowen
February 10 ·

Chronicles of a Brain Tumor Warrior:

It's a God Day! Every day should be one, but those days where I need him the most. He shows up. He is so perfect in all of HIS ways. I struggled this morning. I struggled to get up, to feel better, and to understand just how my body is working. Two spots- one big ole dent that seems to further its impression every. SINGLE. day and then a small little spot that is SO aggravating. They will open/close. I move back and forth bandaging them. From band-aids to gauze to nothing. My skin is starting to break out from the "sticky goo" from the paper tape, the band-aids, etc. My hair gets trapped and it's becoming quite an art to bandage up. Every time they open....I just think there goes 1 more piece of my forehead. My body is fighting where the bone is eroding. Killing it even more. BUT>>>>

God showed up in song. God showed up in messages. God showed up in love. From the ashes I arise. God's soldier. I cannot let the devil get me! NOT TODAY SATAN! God has the healing power and I am HIS DAUGHTER! Here's to my fancy bandaged head today. I can't get lost in the whys or how comes??? I can't let this bring me down. I only know that whatever is happening God has a plan. When I go for my biopsy in March, I know those answers will bring more steps to walk on this journey, but I am not alone. To those that sent the love --- thank you! You don't know how much it helped and turned my day around! Chronicles of a Brain Tumor Warrior- Crystal's Journey

Crystal Gowen

February 20 ·

Chronicles of a Brain Tumor Warrior...

If you could imagine running your fingertips across those weather beaten scars, they'd have a story to tell. In my mind, an old movie reel winding through decades of events- none too big or small- carving, molding, and etching. Welding pieces where I thought I was broken into this beautiful story-page after page- penned by God. For He thinks I'm beautiful even when the reflection I see may not be that of symmetry or flawlessness, He reminds me of the scars and I run my fingertips over them---those markings of character. Chronicles of a Brain Tumor Warrior-Crystal's Journey

My scars tell a story.
They are a reminder of times
when life tried to break me,
but failed.
They are markings of where the
structure of my character was welded.

- Steve Maraboli

© 2015 Nina Dobrev

Crystal Gowen
February 23 ·

Chronicles of a Brain Tumor Warrior ....

Some days the water seems like it's clear up to my neck and I'm quiet to keep from taking on the water. Those are the days I lift up my eyes and pray. I reach out to the Lord and I pray. Sometimes I can't utter words and the tears speak for themselves. Yet, I know God has me. He carries me through the roughest waters, parts the seas, until I reach the shores. Chronicles of a Brain Tumor Warrior- Crystal's Journey

"When you go through deep waters, I will be with you. When you go through rivers of difficulty, you will not drown..."

Isiah 43:2 NLT

Crystal Gowen
March 23 ·

Chronicles of a Brain Tumor Warrior...

My last day at work is today. I'm already missing my people. It's a void when you don't get the chance to talk to your work family on a regular. This medical leave has been different. I've prepared prior to leave like never before. I am grateful for the support and prayers. I'll miss my team tremendously, I already do. From my lips to God's ears, I pray for a good outcome, a swift fight, and blessed recovery. This surgery marks the first step in this new battle. I'm worn, weary, and torn from this journey.....BUT my God is GOOD! Chronicles of a Brain Tumor Warrior- Crystal's Journey

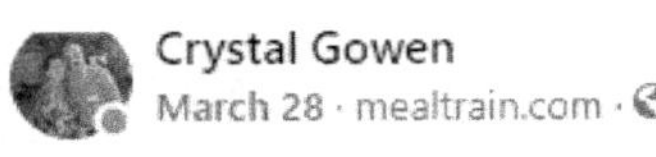

Crystal Gowen
March 28 · mealtrain.com ·

Chronicles of a Brain Tumor Warrior:

Our family cannot express the outpouring support you have shown us as we prepare for this journey. Surgery will be conducted tomorrow afternoon. I hope we can update you tomorrow, before too late, no later than Wednesday. I ask for your continued prayers. Prayer is powerful. Our God is SO very good and has been good to us. Satan might think he has the upper hand, but MY GOD continues to carry me. I will not tarry and I will continue to share all the blessings God has bestowed upon my family and me. Again, thank you SO very much! I cannot express how much this has meant to us.

-Crystal

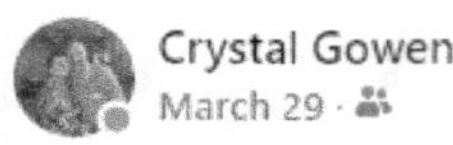

Crystal Gowen
March 29 ·

This has always been one of my favorite wedding pictures. At face value, you see a man and woman, very much in love, on their wedding day embracing for a kiss. The groom dips his wife back, holding her steady, to kiss her longingly.
I look at this picture and see the strength of my husband and how much his arms have carried me, with God's unwavering support, since this day. He is strongly rooted, arms wrapped solidly, with heart entangled around me. His kiss an expression of his love, and yet a seal of promises to come through good times and thunderous storms that wildly mask sunnier days with hard emotions that seem unending. He gives beyond his all, even on days that deplete him. He returns again to face it. On days like today, he is this man and more. Loving and funny. Waiting to dive with me into what lays ahead. Yes, there's more to this picture than what you see.
Please say prayers for my husband. Being strong takes prayer and being on this journey with me takes prayer. He will be alone waiting today and I'm sure in prayer himself....but if you could say prayers for him as well....I would forever appreciate it.

Crystal Gowen
March 30 ·

Chronicles of a Brain 🧠 Tumor Warrior...

Yesterday's surgery went well. I was discharged to return home. The outcome from the surgery is...
1. No biopsy was completed. It was indicative the bone flap is infected all the way through and is not salvageable. Unfortunately, the neurosurgeon was not available to assist to remove the bone flap yesterday. So, I will have to return to remove it. The two teams will convene to determine the best option. There are several. From what I have been told, it's likely two more surgeries will be needed. One to remove the bone flap and another to insert the prosthetic. They will also discuss what to do in light of the other tumor.
2. The surgeon debrided the area as best as possible and sutured the two small areas to assist with the ongoing drainage.
3. Yesterday was rough. I was stuck four times and blew three veins in an attempt to get an IV. I required additional medication to aid with my oxygen stats during surgery. In the meantime, I will need to focus on making changes to keep me hydrated and healthier in preparation for the next upcoming surgeries.
4. I literally feel like someone took steel wool and scraped the inside clean. Coming out of all the meds left me sick and my head hurting. The bandages come off Thursday evening. I have a drain that will likely come out in a week.
5. Emotionally, I'm all over the place. I'm disappointed because I truly was hoping for a less invasive journey. I AM TIRED. This journey is tiring. I'd be lying if I said the contrary. The pain, the multiple surgeries, the second tumor, the constant drainage....my body is tired. I want my Heavenly body and I want the people I miss present so badly, namely my Mom, Papa, and Tim. I miss their grit during times like these.
Yesterday, I wallowed around in these feelings for a while. Others could hear the distress in my voice and I cried out I'm tired. I faced these emotions head on. I admitted they were there and cried out because the load is heavy.
I needed to just for a minute to remind me I couldn't stay in them. I won't lie and say they may not reappear, but I sure needed the Lord to remind me why I can't stay in them and that He continues to carry my load. I have to move forward because God is still writing chapters in my story. My light still needs to shine. My love for God is needed for others. There's a purpose to my presence on this Earth. The people I love need me and I need them.
This recovery is part of an awakening of continued faith and resolve. Big prayers are needed. Please pray for medical teams to find the best possible solution, pray that the pain subsides, pray that my family's worries are calmed, pray that the nausea passes, pray our finances are covered and I'm well enough to return back to the team I love and miss, and pray for my kids who saw a weary Mama cry tonight and whose hearts were heavy for her. Pray because prayer is powerful.
Chronicles of a Brain Tumor Warrior- Crystal's Journey

Crystal Gowen
April 7 ·

Chronicles of a Brain Tumor Warrior

It's been one week since surgery. I had my post-op appointment Tuesday. The surgeon said half of my bone flap (forehead) is necrotic. The blood supply never regained in a previous surgery and the bone has died completely to the brain. In laments terms, that part of the bone is like a sponge. His recommendation is to remove this part of the bone and replace it with a titanium plate in six months. As you know, I have a small tumor in the olfactory groove. In September 21, she had not grown that much. So, my case has been turned back to my neurosurgeon, Dr. Friedman. I will have an MRI and follow up visit with him on 4/19. The surgery could entail removing that tumor if necessary. I pray God performs a miracle and this tumor is not a threat. I pray the blood supply to it is killed off and that the Lord will perform a miracle beyond my own thoughts. We know this means more time from work, and how long we don't know. BUT God will provide. He always has.

Thank you to our family & friends that have brought food so far and continue to do so. Those who are helping us to celebrate Riley's birthday this weekend. Thank you for the calls and texts and the many, many prayers.

Thank you Jackie Burkhalter-Spillman and Chris Spillman for the pot roast the day of surgery. Ensuring the kids and Mama had a meal (and us when we arrived home) was a blessing; to Daddy & Gail for Chicken pastry, Chicken salad, fried chicken, sides, and dessert last Wednesday, especially when my jaw was so sore and I needed comfort food; to my sister, Brandie Black for ensuring we had had a meal last Thursday because soup is just what I needed; to Deanne Scott Worrell and Jody Worrell for the cabbage, potatoes, and smoked sausage...it was delicious; to Lucy Hooper for the meatloaf, sides, and dessert... The cornbread was the best; to Beth Medlin and Jeramy for the Italian pasta dish...it was a hit and we loved it; to Sandy Harris for the salad and bread sticks we added to our pasta leftovers and made another meal and for the conversation I needed; to Brenda Conney Holton Norman, Briana Moore Madison Holton and Garrett Moore for the chicken pot pie..we enjoyed it very much and appreciate the prayers; and to Monique Lee for supper tonight and the beautiful prayer you prayed over me and my family. I wanted to recognize you all for taking time to take care of my family and me. We look forward to the donated meals ahead of us and cannot wait to enjoy in your company. Chronicles of a Brain Tumor Warrior- Crystal's Journey

Crystal Gowen
April 14 ·

Chronicles of a Brain 🧠 Tumor Warrior...

Tuesday, April 19th I'll be undergoing my next surgery (#5) to remove my bone flap (forehead) as it is infected (isolated to that area) and Dr. Friedman doesn't want it to spread and make me sick. This unknown journey, losing my bone flap and having a disfigurement (while temporary) is a lot to cope with. I'm blessed by God to have a wonderful support system of family and friends. I know God will provide and never forsake me. Please continue to pray for us.

Crystal Gowen
April 17 ·

Chronicles of a Brain Tumor Warrior....

Dr. Friedman's team has just called this evening due to a cancellation he had for tomorrow. Surgery will be tomorrow - early afternoon. Please say prayers as I wrap my mind around this procedure- a day early. I know I didn't have to go ahead and do it, but God led me to say yes. No matter the day, He will be there. He's picking up my sword and I'm relying on his arm to the light of His face to get me through this. He has heard my cries, recorded every tear I've shed, and by his stripes I will be healed. Amen! Chronicles of a Brain Tumor Warrior- Crystal's Journey

Crystal Gowen
April 18 ·

Chronicles of a Brain 🧠 Tumor Warrior....

When your neurosurgeon autographs your forehead.

Still waiting in pre-op. Thank you all for the prayers, texts, and support. God has this!! He's recorded my tears today, my prayers, and my praises.

He, God, makes it happen.
From the parking spot; seeing Mrs. Ellen Jones Gray and that hug this morning; the wonderful staff in pre-op, prayers via text, phone, and Facebook; reading in Psalms this morning accounting each time David praised God, God kept him upright, and every promise God made to handle this; blessed with time with my husband; playing my Christian worship music - thinking of the songs Teri Thompson has introduced to me over the years that bring me peace; and the overwhelming unending faithfulness of my God.

Thess. 5:16-17 Rejoice always pray continuously.

This is the day the Lord has made and even in this time, I will be glad in it. Chronicles of a Brain Tumor Warrior- Crystal's Journey

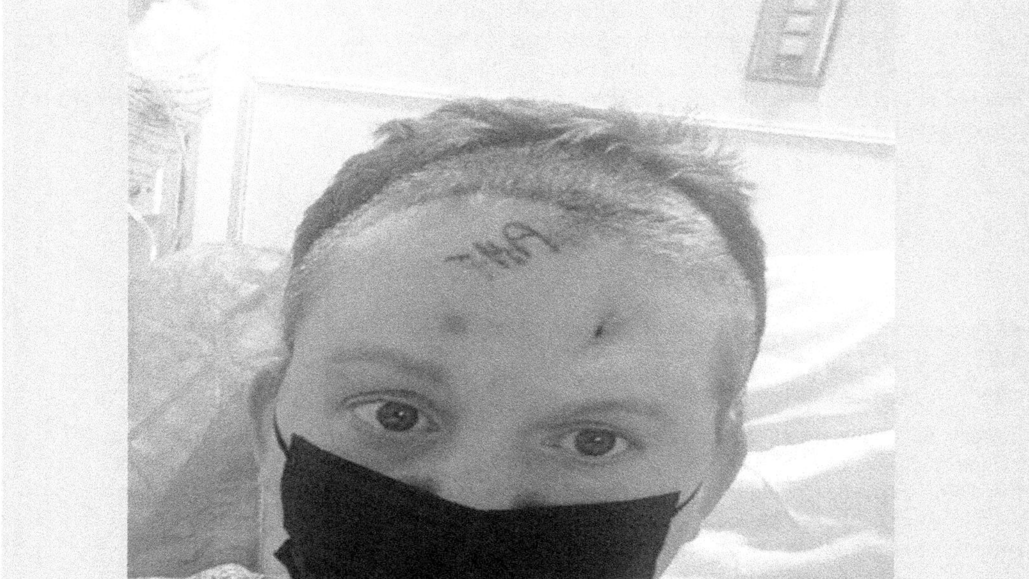

Crystal Gowen
April 19 ·

Chronicles of a Brain 🧠 Tumor Warrior...

Can I get a Hallelujah?!?!?!

The Lord has brought me through another surgery. It was hard y'all. Hard on my mind creating a storm of depression and anxiety; hard on my heart as this journey is tiresome and I had grown so weary; hard on my soul as the devil tried his best to cast me in a pit of worry, deceive me about the promises God made, and cast doubt about what my Lord could do.

It was hard in recovery, mentally, because I could feel myself slipping, BUT as my cousin, Brandy Edwards Duke , says BIG Daddy Jesus won't about to let me fall in that abyss. Once I was transferred to my room, it's like the manna fell from Heaven, rocks were cracked and water flowed...and my Lord grabbed my hand and said you're not going to fall... I'm right here. I found joy and rejoiced in the day the Lord made.

They removed my bandages and this is my dressing. While I haven't seen the exact finished product, I'm told it looks good. Y'all I imagined something totally different, something I didn't think I would be able to cope with and by all means this isn't vanity. I worried I wouldn't be able to cope with going out in public and had pretty much made my mind up I'd be home the next six months, BUT God blessed me PERIOD. Even if it was worse, I'm still ready to let it be my testimony...let it be seen....for folks to know how many times God has SAVED me.

Cameron read me messages/texts and relayed to me phone conversations. I'm overwhelmed to say the least. I know I've got to take more steps in this journey, but God has provided me with an abundance of love and support. Thank y'all so much for your prayers and love. Chronicles of a Brain Tumor Warrior- Crystal's Journey

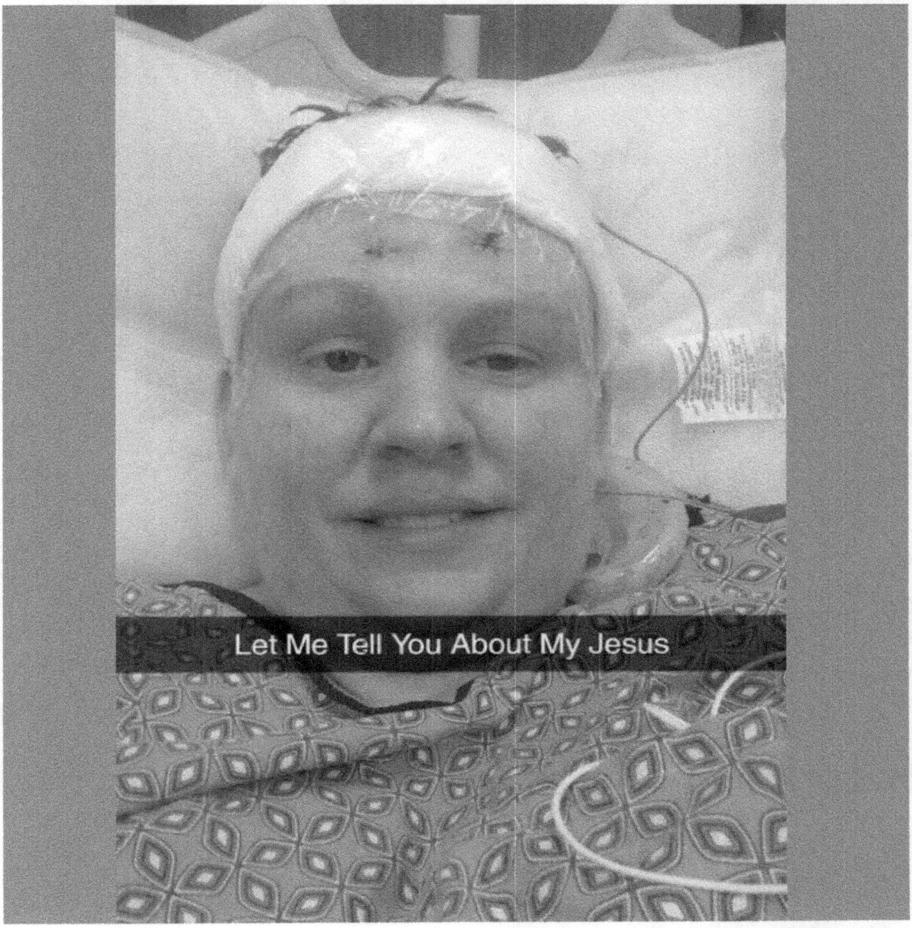

Crystal Gowen

April 19 ·

Please keep those prayers coming....

I've had my head molded for the plastic piece to wear for the next 6 months. I have met with Infectious Disease and thus far no PICC line-- only antibiotics by mouth. We pray this continues and no other germs grow and no PICC line is needed. We pray that discharge can remain for tomorrow as we know hospital staff has begun working on it. We pray the pain subsides and the IV team can find good veins until discharge for my IV meds. We give praise to God for the blessings He has bestowed!!! Chronicles of a Brain Tumor Warrior- Crystal's Journey

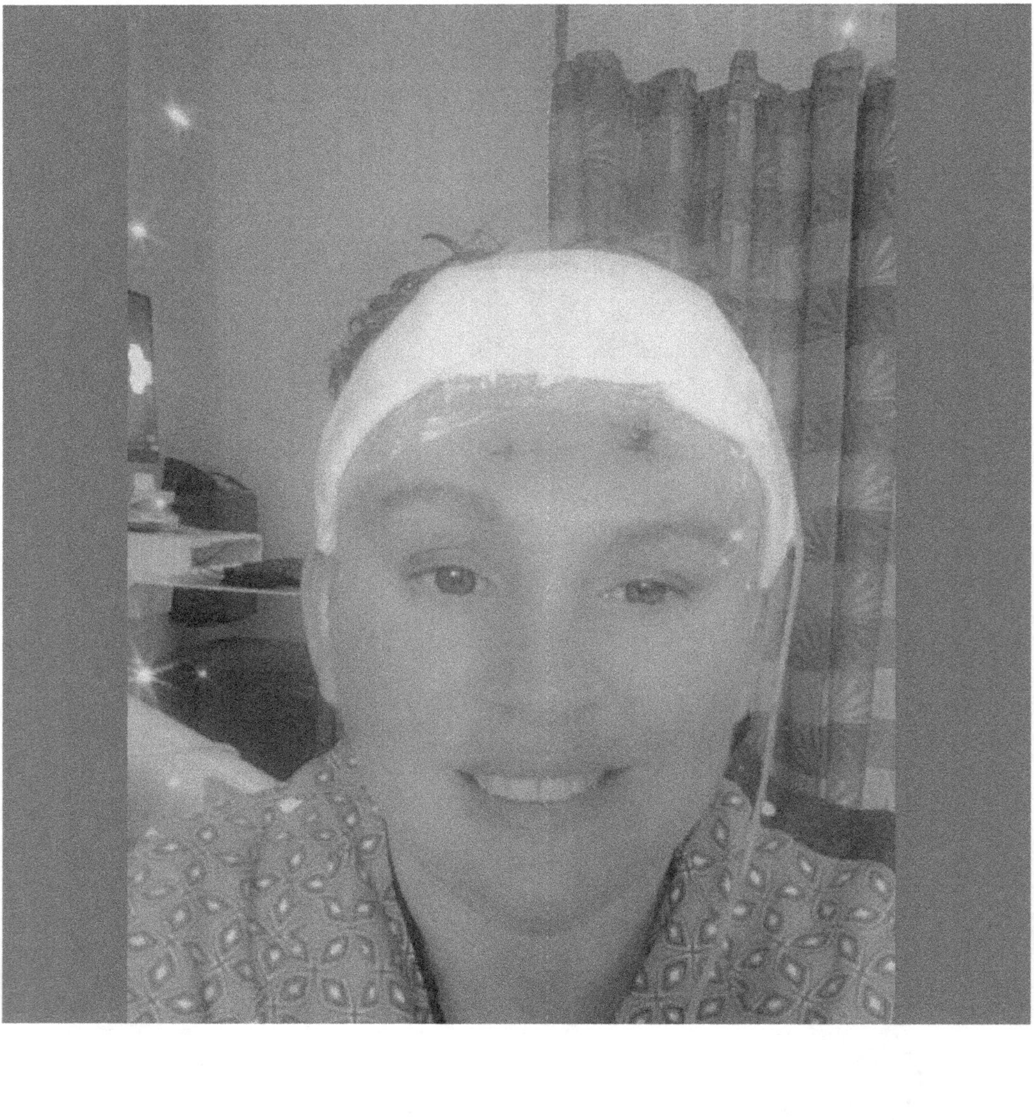

Crystal Gowen
April 25 ·

. Lord....bring me this peace.

BE SO CONFIDENT IN GOD'S PLAN THAT YOU DON'T EVEN GET UPSET ANYMORE WHEN THINGS DON'T GO YOUR WAY.

@_SHE_RISES_

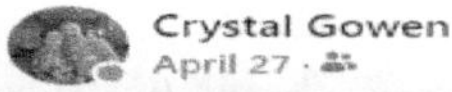

Crystal Gowen
April 27 ·

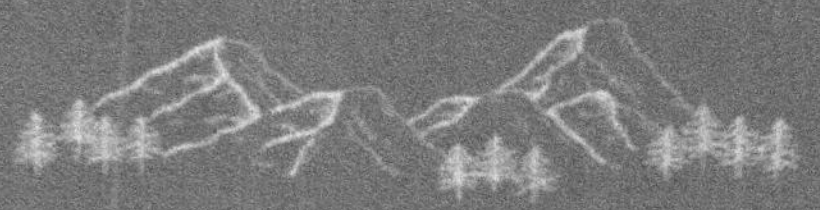

GOD DIDN'T ALWAYS MOVE THE MOUNTAIN, BUT DAY BY DAY, HE PROVIDED ME WITH ENOUGH GRACE TO CLIMB IT.

#GrowingSlow
@JenniferDukesLee

Crystal Gowen
April 30 ·

Lord....I'm trying.

I need a WORD
April 30 ·

Spiritual maturity is when you can say His timing, not mine.

Crystal Gowen
May 4 ·

Chronicles of a Brain 🧠 Tumor Warrior...

We go gray in May to support Brain Cancer/Tumor Awareness. This journey is far from easy, physically or emotionally, especially on those that are our caregivers/family/friends. They fight as strongly as we do. Their prayers, support, and love are neverending and remain steadfast, even when we feel lost or just plain tired. This is an exhausting journey and it's full of ups and downs, but it comes with many blessings even through the weariness. God has blessed me tremendously and while I'm still battling with fearing the unknown, I know God has a plan for me. I may not like all the twists or turns or even the outcomes, but God is faithful.

Please help me honor all of us who endure this journey (by wearing gray, checking in, or making a donation to support research) and for those whose journey has come to and end with our Lord. They are forever healed and in Heaven. We will see them one day and O, what a day that will be!!! Until then, we fight this battle!!!

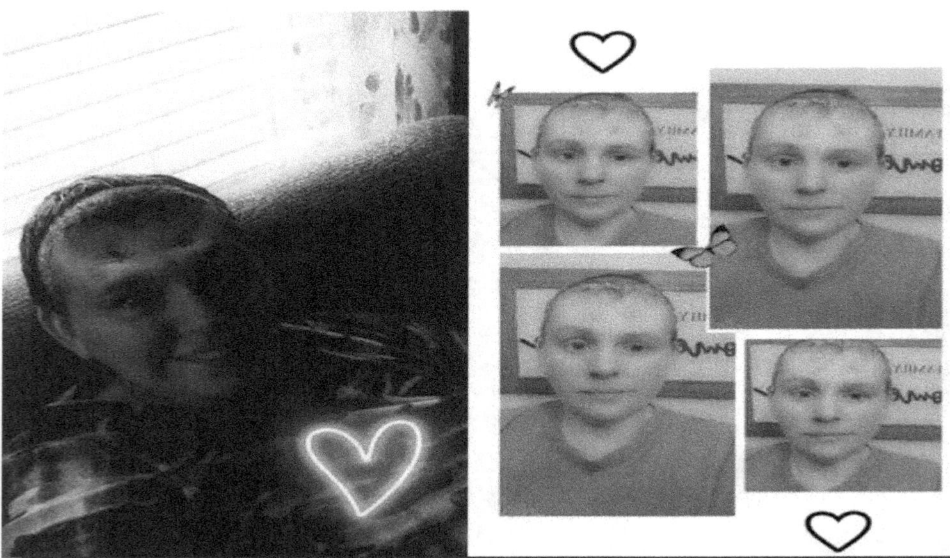

Chronicles of a Brain Tumor Warrior....

God doesn't give us a spirit of fear, but one of power, love, and self control.

This got me through a tedious suture removal today. Praise the Lord I have healed so well, there were difficult ones to remove. With each removal of those hard to remove ones, I lifted my hands and praised God. I praised Him for remov ng my stitches, even though at times it caused me discomfort. I know the Lord is working on my spirit to refrain from worry and fear. Today, I woke up and conversed with God, throughout the drive to Duke, and I prayed for the nurses as they struggled and felt bad because they knew it had to hurt. They asked me for breaks, but I asked to push forward. Why? I knew my God had this. He had me. He knew how this story would be written and I trusted Him to know He always has what's in my best interest. I'm humbled our God loves me enough to tend to me, to be right there, giving me courage to press on when I would have usually become fearful and worried. I'm ecstatic I could do this for the Lord! I give Him all the glory and praise. Thank you Jesus! Chronicles of a Brain Tumor Warrior- Crystal's Journey

Crystal Gowen
May 29 ·

Chronicles of a Brain Tumor Warrior...

Prayer is one of the most important aspects of my relationship with God. I literally pray EVERYwhere. I pray for family, friends, special prayer requests, relationships, and I pray for myself just as Jesus did in the garden before being betrayed and arrested. I give God all the glory in my life. He IS the author of my story from cover to cover. As I am reading His from cover to cover, I find myself convicted to seek my purpose, to understand my story, to increase my faith, to understand His will on things my mind can't comprehend. I struggle to understand the loss of people I love so soon, afflictions tormenting the bodies of people I love, the senseless taking of lives, the pain I see in the world around me. I believe in God's love. It is a powerful emotion that can bring me crumbling into tears of joy. I'm not a perfect person. Every day I know I probably sin, but I don't intend to...rather my intentions are to be after God's own heart just like David. So, this message tonight is not one of boasting, BUT one of faith and salvation. I encourage you to seek the Lord, commit your life to Him, and find the greatest love of all. There's NOT one thing He can't do. Chronicles of a Brain Tumor Warrior- Crystal's Journey

Too Good To Not Believe

Brandon Lake, Jenn Johnson

Crystal Gowen shared a memory.
June 11 ·

Chronicles of a Brain 🧠 Tumor Warrior...

Reading this three years later, I am taken back to those emotions. They will always be raw, yet I don't stay "in" them because my journey has brought me farther. God knew where I'd be today before I could fathom it. I have been a God believing woman, but I've evolved since then. I was the one he searched out from the ninety-nine. Five surgeries later (waiting for the sixth and LAST one-- I'm claiming it), my flesh has been tested and my spirit renewed. I have failed Him many times during this journey....when I wanted to give up, He wouldn't let me...He never gave up on me. He has pulled me out of the dark huddled corners of anxiety and depression I have battled and continue to battle. He has loved me SO much more than the love I can give myself. The grace he has circumvented in my life that I still to this day am humbled by and by no means deserve as a sinner....
God, I'm so grateful for every day you carried me; took my heavy yoked burden (even when I didn't want to give it to you because I thought I needed to control it); every worship song sung, messaged, and played; every prayer prayed on my behalf; blessings bestowed; weapons formed against me that DID NOT prosper; the healing from the top of my head to the soles of my feet; those who anointed me; and the love I have sought that you unselfishly gave through your Son, Jesus Christ. Thank you for this journey that has brought your prodigal child home. Please continue to keep me covered in your hedge of protection. Surround me with strength to fight battles and return home to you always until my name is called. Let Your light shine through me as I give You all the glory and praise...may I be less of me and more of You.
Chronicles of a Brain Tumor Warrior- Crystal's Journey
-Amen

3 Years Ago

See your memories >

Crystal Gowen

June 11, 2019 ·

You never know what can happen in life. I was just at a concert and took a fall. The fall was caused by a spilled beverage on concrete steps. I didn't expect to be faced with a brain tumor (olfactory meniginoma- typically the largest intracranial brain tumor) before my 40th birthday approaches. Here I am... I'm facing a tumor about 4 cm and we've named him Ted. Mostly to provide some humor to our situation and to keep us all sane. Today, my surgeon at Duke has decided to give Ted his eviction notice on June 20th. I will go June 19th for pre-op and be admitted. Ted can't live here any longer. He's simply too big and while I've not had a symptom yet, I don't want any. God has brought me here and I've struggled. I've struggled with faith and trying to keep my anxiety at bay. I've struggled with feeling like I should have more faith than I do. I've struggled with the overwhelming sensation of how quickly this has happened. I've shed tears, paced, and been fearful. Yet my testimony is this...God has not forsaken me. He's brought forth witnesses to remind me I am a child of God and to profess my faith, and it is not a lost faith. Why?! Because my God knew even before I did what I would need. Continue to pray for my husband, kids, and family. Pray for my team at Duke. Pray for me. #evictted Brain Tumor Warrior- Crystal's Journey

Crystal Gowen
August 23 ·

Chronicles of a Brain Tumor Warrior.....

This right here breaks my "earthly" heart, while my soul rejoices that she's free... Free of cancer and all that entails. God pens our stories for His purpose and in her story... her testimony....her Big Daddy Jesus light shined so bright for all to see. I saw faith and love encapsulate with every word she blogged. She inspired as she praised God. God has written an amazing story in her life and will continue through her testimony as we all share it.

"He will wipe away every tear from their eyes, and death shall be no more, neither shall there be mourning, nor crying, nor pain anymore, for the former things have passed away" – Romans 8:1

"Blessed are those who mourn, for they will be comforted" – Matthew 5:4

"Those who have been ransomed by the Lord will return. They will enter Jerusalem singing, crowned with everlasting joy. Sorrow and mourning will disappear, and they will be filled with joy and gladness" – Isaiah 51:11

"Blessed be the God and Father of our Lord Jesus Christ, the Father of mercies and God of all comfort, who comforts us in all our affliction, so that we may be able to comfort those who are in any affliction, with the comfort with which we ourselves are comforted by God" – Corinthians 1:3

"Though he brings grief, he will show compassion, so great is his unfailing love." - Lamentations 3:32

Chronicles of a Brain Tumor Warrior- Crystal's Journey

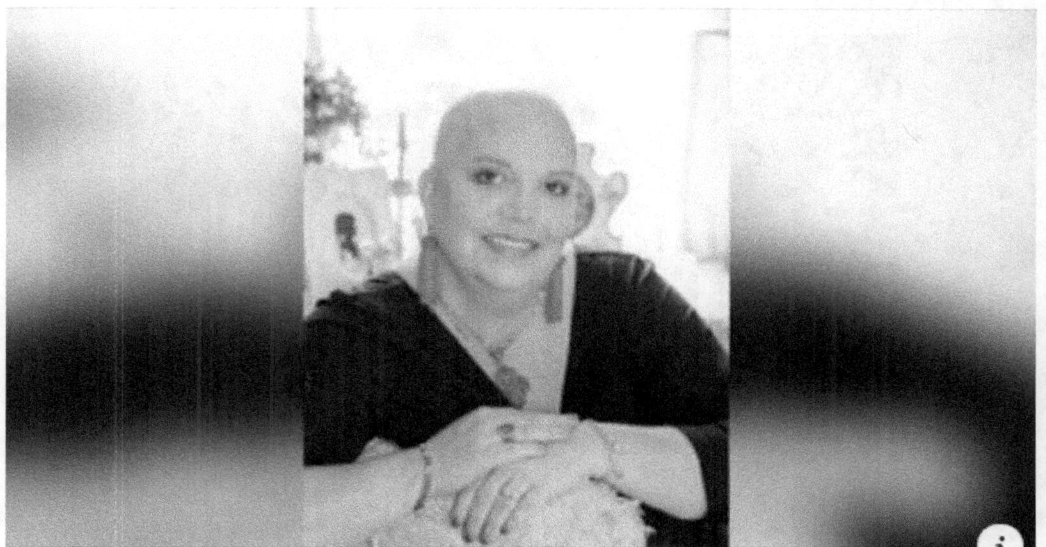

Crystal Gowen
September 1 ·

Chronicles of a Brain Tumor Warrior...
It's September Y'ALL!!!
For years this month signaled fall, family, and food. Nowadays, it also signals my yearly MRI scan. There's still a small brain tumor there. Last year, it was the size of a pea. This year, I am claiming my GOD will heal me. He will keep it from growing or banish it altogether. Jesus already took up our infirmities and bore our diseases (Isaiah 53:4), so I know it is already HANDLED. The page has been written and I will be okay. I just don't know the journey. That's the hardest part sometimes to accept, but God told us we must be faithful. I have prayed earnestly and at times desperately that this brain tumor will no longer grow. Dr. Friedman told me in May if it doesn't grow, we will wait and watch. Some of them have been known not to grow and in some cases go away. If it does grow, he's thinking "spot on" radiation.
I'm facing another surgery, too. That titanium forehead will be back just in time for Christmas (I hope). It'll be another season in this journey of surgery and recovery. It takes its toll on my body. It's the third one this year.
You know Jesus died for me; taking on this entire journey in His suffering. I have to find joy in my journey. It's the best medicine for me. He never said I would like it or that it would be easy, but I sure am glad He thinks enough of me to be by my side and to place those who love, care, and pray for me.
So, if y'all would throw up some prayers to my BIG DADDY JESUS as my cousin, Brandy Edwards Duke would say. (She's there with our Lord completely healed.) Pray for this tumor to remain stable. Pray for no radiation. Pray for an uncomplicated surgery. Pray that my hardest days don't succumb to worry as I grasp my mustard seed tightly. Pray I find joy in each of my days. Pray.
Chronicles of a Brain Tumor Warrior- Crystal's Journey

Crystal Gowen
September 21 at 12:26 PM ·

Chronicles of a Brain Tumor Warrior...

Yesterday, I broke for a moment. Sometimes the devil tries his best to sneak in and break me and shroud my spirit with anxiety. No matter how much he tries, y'all my JESUS is SO much BIGGER. The devil will not SHAKE me! MRIs, reports, meeting with doctors, the what ifs, and what comes nexts are all so daunting. So, yeah I let those tears slide down my cheeks. I let those emotions just cry out to MY God and he bottled each and EVERY. SINGLE. ONE. OF. THEM. And His Spirit just calmed me. Whatever the outcome, whatever the treatment plan, whatever....I'm His. He is my rock, my foundation, and my Waymaker.

Chronicles of a Brain Tumor Warrior- Crystal's Journey

Chronicles of a Brain Tumor Warrior- Crystal's Journey
September 22 at 1:48 PM ·

Chronicles of a Brain 🧠 Tumor Warrior...
(previous post)
This "helmet" sits on my dresser and when I brought it home 6 weeks ago, it was the epitome of every grueling disappointment through this journey. It was the detour of all detours. It meant a piece of me was missing.
I loathed it.
I feared it.
I wanted to run from it.

Six weeks later, it's still on my dresser. It's part of my ensemble daily. It's no longer the epitome of a disheartened journey, but one of "power, love and sound mind."
Now it's part of my daily armor.
It symbolizes hope.
It's embedded in faith.
It symbolizes a journey of love.... God's love.

Family & Friends,

I learned these things on my post-op visit Tuesday,

1. My incision is healing well. It's impressive and there are no further concerns.
2. I am linked to another surgeon, Dr. Powers, who will assist Dr. Friedman in six months to complete the cranioplasty and God will bless me with a titanium plate.
3. My "helmet" attire (skull cap, helmet, fashionable cap over it) was impressive to my doctor.
4. My annual MRI is in September. If the reoccurring tumor does not grow, we wait and watch it. (It's small). If it does, he will likely radiate to prevent further surgeries.
My God is the Almighty Physician and I know He will heal me (it'll go away- they've been known to do that- or He will make a way for me to be healed. He already knows the ending to this journey. I just gotta be still.)
5. Every day my body has NO longer had that missing piece, has been one where I have felt better physically.
6. Every day I walk with the Lord continues to bring me closer to Him.

Ephesians 6:10-18

10 Finally, be strong in the Lord and in his mighty power. 11 Put on the full armor of God, so that you can take your stand against the devil's schemes. 12 For our struggle is not against flesh and blood,but against the rulers, against the authorities,against the powers of this dark world and against the spiritual forces of evil in the heavenly realms.13 Therefore put on the full armor of God, so that when the day of evil comes, you may be able to stand your ground, and after you have done everything, to stand. 14 Stand firm then, with the belt of truth buckled around your waist, with the breastplate of righteousness in place, 15 and with your feet fitted with the readiness that comes from the gospel of peace. 16 In addition to all this, take up the shield of faith, with which you can extinguish all the flaming arrows of the evil one. 17 Take the helmet of salvation and the sword of the Spirit, which is the word of God.

18 And pray in the Spirit on all occasions with all kinds of prayers and requests. With this in mind, be alert and always keep on praying for all the Lord's people

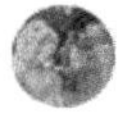

Chronicles of a Brain Tumor Warrior- Crystal's Journey
September 24 at 11:12 AM ·

God,

Thank you for blessing me with the time to make memories with these three. I miss Mama and Riley and wish they could be with us. Yet, I have learned on this journey to find the grace in every thing. Every trial, tribulation, and struggle has an unseen reflection of grace in the end. It's beautiful just like these three that I am blessed to see smiling in the reflection back to me. Thank you God for giving this ole sinner the grace I need every day, making preparations for what lies ahead, and loving me... especially in the moments I couldn't love myself. #childofGod

Crystal Gowen is with **Brandie Black** and **4 others**.
September 27 at 8:17 AM ·

Prayer Warriors,
Please say a prayer today. I have my annual MRI scan to check on the reoccurring tumor today. I will get my results and meet my new plastic surgeon that will assist my neurosurgeon with the titanium plate to replace my forehead. I praise God this morning, giving Him all the glory, for without Him I would not be where I am in this journey.

"Heal me, O Lord, and I will be healed; save me and I will be saved, for you are the one I praise." ~ Jeremiah 17:14

"Is anyone among you sick? Let them call the elders of the church to pray over them and anoint them with oil in the name of the Lord. And the prayer offered in faith will make the sick person well; the Lord will raise them up. If they have sinned, they will be forgiven." ~ James 5:14-15

Chronicles of a Brain Tumor Warrior- Crystal's Journey

Crystal Gowen is with **Brandie Black** and **3 others**.
September 28 at 1:38 PM ·

Chronicles of a Brain Tumor 🧠 Warrior

Yesterday wasn't the news I expected. There's another tumor present over my left orbit. This makes two tumors. The original (ethmoid area) tumor has not grown, SO I praise God for answering that prayer! Both tumors are small, but the left orbit tumor is bigger than the other one and Dr. Friedman prefers it removed now rather than later. Dr. Powers reviewed the titanium plate and recovery procedure. However, the additional surgical procedure to remove the tumor creates more risks and recovery time. I know God is with me and that's one thing I learned from my cousin, Brandy Edwards Duke. I have a scheduled CT scan next Tuesday to obtain the measurements for the titanium plate. It takes about 2-3 weeks for it to come back and surgery should occur mid-end October. More information to come. Please keep our family in your prayers. Today, we celebrate my husband's birthday. I'm giving it to God because I won't be the stumbling blocks ahead of the blessings He will bestow upon me. Follow me for more updates at: Chronicles of a Brain Tumor Warrior- Crystal's Journey

The road I've traveled hasn't been easy, but I'm still here. The only reason I'm here today is because God was walking the road with me, every step of the way.

Crystal Gowen is at **Duke Health (Duke Raleigh Hospital Imaging Services)**.
October 4 at 10:50 AM · Raleigh ·

Chronicles of a Brain Tumor Warrior- Crystal's Journey CT scan to get this titanium "part" ordered to match. God, I pray this scan goes well and there won't be any complications. Thank you for Cameron and this time we have in these appointments. #findingjoyinmyjourney

Crystal Gowen
October 9 at 9:25 AM ·

Hunt High Class Of '97 Warriors!!! Reunion weekend was a blast! Pre-gaming with my besties and hubby to dancing the night away with my classmates. The laughter and love captured memories and a night to remember. My timeline is flooded this a.m. with pictures! Here's a few from us to share. Living my best life in the midst of my Chronicles of a Brain Tumor Warrior- Crystal's Journey and y'all made it amazing!!! Thank you to everyone who worked so hard to make the reunion a great time!!! Hunt High School 25th Class Reunion

Chronicles of a Brain Tumor Warrior- Crystal's Journey

14h ·

Finding joy in the journey?!?! What does this mean? For me, it's finding the joy in the most bittersweet of moments. It's finding joy in the most heart wrenching moments. It's knowing God is in both. My smile 😊 is there, not only because I'm joyful, but because true joy comes from God. In the midst of this three year journey, there is pain, both physical and emotional; raw days where I can't remember who I was before it all began and who I'm becoming with each step; and struggles to see the ending I constantly pray for to God. Yet, I know there's an ending far more glorious than I'll ever imagine. There's joy to be had in moments here and now. Simply there's joy.

Today, my joy is found in the smallest nooks and crannies. It radiates through the sunshine while I drive Gracie to school, Mama rejoicing she's found her TV remote, Cameron being the morning person he is, Ashleighs's mischievous smile, and Riley's protective nature over his Mama. Each day I'm presented, I seek the joy...and yes some days are harder than others. Yet, I find as we wait in the call to surgery from Duke, there's much to be joyous about. Crystal Gowen

Chronicles of a Brain Tumor Warrior- Crystal's Journey
1d ·

It matters not if the world has heard or approves or understands...the only applause we're meant to seek is that of nail-scarred hands.

Bj Hoff

meetville.com

www.ingramcontent.com/pod-product-compliance
Lightning Source LLC
LaVergne TN
LVHW010607160826
845677LV00013B/3285

* 9 7 9 8 3 5 7 9 6 7 1 8 3 *